New policies for older workers

Philip Taylor

First published in Great Britain in December 2002 by

The Policy Press
34 Tyndall's Park Road
Bristol BS8 1PY
UK

Tel no +44 (0)117 954 6800
Fax no +44 (0)117 973 7308
E-mail tpp-info@bristol.ac.uk
www.policypress.org.uk

© University of Cambridge 2002

Published for the Joseph Rowntree Foundation by The Policy Press

ISBN 1 86134 463 5

Philip Taylor is a Senior Research Associate in and Executive Director of the Cambridge Interdisciplinary Research Centre on Ageing (CIRCA), University of Cambridge.

The **Joseph Rowntree Foundation** has supported this project as part of its programme of research and innovative development projects, which it hopes will be of value to policy makers, practitioners and service users. The facts presented and views expressed in this report are, however, those of the author and not necessarily those of the Foundation.

Photograph on front cover supplied by PhotoDisc
Cover design by Qube Design Associates, Bristol
Printed in Great Britain by Hobbs the Printers Ltd, Southampton

Contents

Acknowledgements

The author is grateful to Mark Hinman, Donald Hirsch and Lynne Spence at the Joseph Rowntree Foundation for their help and support. He is also grateful to the members of the project's advisory committee – Robert Anderson, Christine Ashdown, Ross Brown, Elizabeth Farmer, Patrick Grattan, Tony Maltby, Samantha Mercer and Fritz von Nordheim-Nielsen – for their advice and support. In addition he is grateful to the considerable number of individuals who gave their time to be interviewed or helped the project in other ways.

Summary

In recent years consideration of the needs of older workers has moved up the policy agenda in the UK. Since the late 1980s there has been an increasing emphasis on overcoming age barriers and extending working life. Likewise, policy making in this area is developing in other countries and, in some, policies have existed for a considerable time. Thus, there is potential value in observing and drawing lessons from policy making elsewhere.

This report examines developments in public policies on age and employment in Australia, Finland, Germany, Japan, the Netherlands and the USA. These countries have been chosen because they include countries in which policy making is arguably most established – Finland, Japan and the USA – and countries in which policy making is now emerging. Labour force participation rates are highest in Japan, followed by the USA. They have been considerably lower in the other countries surveyed. Arguably, structural reforms in Germany and Japan's long recession have tempered the development of policies.

Taking as its starting point the suggested need to integrate public policies in this area, this project examined a broad range of policy areas: pension reform, equality, social security and labour market policy.

Policy making on age and employment is perhaps most developed in Australia, Finland and Japan, and least developed in the USA, although some countries are more developed in some areas of public policy than others. Key drivers of public policies have been concerns about labour shortages (Finland, Japan), concerns about the funding of public pensions (Japan, USA) and the recognition of age as an equality issue (Australia, the Netherlands, USA). The integrated approach to policy making is perhaps most developed in Finland. Elsewhere, policies are fragmented. While the need for integration is recognised, this has proved difficult to achieve in practice. Arguably, this has been relatively easy in Finland because of the country's small population.

Turning to the impact of public policies, it was clear from the research that the UK has a better track record of evaluation than several of the countries surveyed; it is simply not possible to make statements regarding the effectiveness of some policies because they have not been systematically evaluated. However, three broad statements can be made:

- *First*, the abolition of mandatory retirement appears to have done little so far to change patterns of retirement. Early retirement is still popular among older workers and employers find other ways of dismissing older workers.
- *Second*, despite their popularity with policy makers, employment subsidies seem to be of limited use, except perhaps where paid to the worker directly. Arguably, schemes aimed at encouraging the employment of older workers through, for example, financial incentives and re-employment schemes, run the risk of deepening age prejudices still further and of institutionalising discrimination against older workers. While some have argued for schemes aimed at encouraging employers to hire older workers on temporary or part-time contracts, these may simply disadvantage those seeking permanent full-time positions and may encourage firms to consider reducing the wages of older workers in the expectation of obtaining a subsidy.

- *Third*, those evaluations that have been undertaken have been quite limited and have not tended to consider displacement and deadweight effects. While the success of programmes aimed at older workers is often heralded in the literature, their real effectiveness is often unclear. Certainly, in terms of the sheer numbers of older workers offered assistance, it is often difficult to see in policy terms why particular schemes have remained in place for so long. The USA's Senior Community Service Employment Program (SCSEP) is a case in point, as it assists only a tiny fraction of the eligible population of older people.

Recommendations for public policy

Policy making on age and employment is in its infancy and models and frameworks for the development of policies are only just emerging. Yet there is much that can be learned from existing initiatives. The following sections attempt to set out some basic principles for the development of policies on age and employment.

Adequate resources for active measures

First, it is clear from this study that extending work life will not be cost neutral. Some older people face multiple barriers that will require an intensive, and therefore costly intervention, for example, those with disabilities or those who have been out of the labour market for a long period. While encouraging the employment of older workers will result in cost savings in terms of pension and social security benefits and increased tax revenues, this will be offset by training and placement costs. Many employers will be reluctant to carry the cost burden of retraining older workers and redesigning workplaces, particularly when they can source cheaper labour from elsewhere.

Integrated/strategic

The need for the integration of public policies on age and employment is emphasised in this report. However, where perhaps even the most integrated initiatives have been deficient is in terms of taking chronological age as their starting point. There would be considerable value in policy on age being integrated with others areas of public policy. For example, there is a need to consider ageing policy alongside those on lifelong learning, the family and labour force diversity more generally. Age issues should be mainstreamed and become part of the activities of all areas of government.

Pension reform has been the driver of much of the policy making in this area and this has often been undertaken without consideration to the implications for employment policy.

Non-age specific

Policy makers have frequently aimed to develop programmes for 'older workers'. This oversimplifies the situation and is paradoxical, given that it is age barriers that are being considered. An approach based on the promotion of 'age diversity' may have greater value. Public programmes that use chronological age as a selection criterion may not send the appropriate message to employers and workers. Definitions such as 'older workers' are almost entirely arbitrary.

It is often hard to see much in programmes that purport to be meeting the needs of older workers that would not also be seen in programmes targeting other groups. Also, age discrimination is not only experienced by people aged over 50, and if many of the disadvantages facing older workers are the same as they have faced throughout their adult lives, it is difficult to argue for age group specific labour market programmes. Instead, there may be greater value in identifying and removing age barriers from within existing initiatives and taking a more positive life course approach. This shifts the emphasis away from developing specific older workers initiatives. More generally, the current fragmentation of policy responses, which, paradoxically, has often resulted in a range of very similar initiatives targeting different 'disadvantaged' groups, has been inefficient and may have weakened their effectiveness.

On occasions, specific support for a particular age cohort may be warranted, but careful consideration must be given to how policies are delivered and promoted if stigmatisation is to be avoided and 'age-aware' employment practices encouraged.

At the same time, age-aware employment requires policy makers to consider the removal of specific employment protection for older workers and to reduce the cost of employing them via the ending of seniority systems. That is not to say, however, that all employment protection should be removed, simply that workers should receive the same level of protection regardless of age, including those beyond the normal age of retirement/state pension age.

Localised/bottom-up

While national government will set the tone for policies towards older workers in terms of incentive structures and employment policy, regional and local government, employer groups, trades unions and organisations working on age issues all have a crucial role to play. In order to appear relevant, campaigns should perhaps be specific and local, and undertaken in collaboration with and working through groups representing sectors, occupations, the trades unions, groups campaigning on age issues and community-based organisations. Moreover, considerably more could be achieved in terms of 'reach' by working through such bodies. This approach will often be perceived to have greater credibility and thus will have greater impact than those in which government is seen to take the lead. The main roles of government here are as sponsor, facilitator, coordinator and provider of information, rather than implementer. Also, employer and trades unions groups could be encouraged to develop comprehensive policies on age and employment separate from their involvement in government committees working on this issue.

Unemployed and disabled older workers are often among the most difficult groups to reach. This suggests that programmes should primarily be offered on an outreach basis or near to the target group.

For companies this means that ready-made solutions brought from outside will generally be of less value than solutions that, with support, are identified from within and 'owned' by the firm. This will necessitate programmes aimed at working with individual firms directly or through sector bodies. Codes of practice and guides to best practice will be of limited value, except as the starting point for discussions in firms.

Targeted

Another feature of public policies on age diversity is that they need to consider the diverse needs of various groups. It has been argued that policy makers must be wary of policies that target heterogeneous groups such 'older workers'. Instead, policies should be nuanced. Consideration should be given to gender, disability, socioeconomic group, occupation and sector of employment.

In raising awareness of age issues, consideration should also be given to the widely differing needs of different industrial sectors.

Flexible

One of the most important features of policy making on age and the labour market should be that it provides people with a degree of choice. For example, there is a danger that pension reforms aimed at extending working life may disadvantage the less well off, forcing them to remain economically active, while the better off will continue to retire early. In order to be successful, public policies must be capable of meeting the needs of different groups. Thus, it is important that an adequate safety net is available to those for whom employment is an unrealistic option.

Preventive

Most, but not all, programmes identified for this study have focused on tackling the issues confronting older workers. This is almost certainly too late in some cases, although it is acknowledged that safety nets are essential. In workplaces, preventive support might include grants for implementing job redesign in order to reduce the risk of disability among workers of all ages and make work more attractive to older workers, and more general consultancy support aimed at improving workplace policy making on age. A particular focus here should be smaller firms without human resource functions. Grants or tax incentives for organisations that implement ergonomic improvements could be offered.

A further approach is to increase labour market flexibility, which would enable workers to move to less demanding jobs.

Tested/evaluated

While some results of the evaluations of initiatives that have been undertaken appear encouraging, questions remain about why initiatives are effective and whether there are displacement and deadweight effects[1]. The literature on the impact of employment programmes more generally is limited by the earlier absence of programmes targeting older workers or their inclusion in more general programmes.

Long-term, consistent and positive

With the erosion of the certainty of fixed retirement ages, there is a need for increased support for older workers in managing risk in terms of career and retirement planning, and obtaining advice and guidance in terms of job-seeking and training. At the same time, planning will be aided by clarity and consistency in social security provision and pension policies.

It is also necessary to get the incentive structure right, and to link this to employment policy so that older workers are encouraged and supported to remain economically active. Pension and employment policy must proceed together if optimal effects are to be achieved.

Consistent, clear and positive messages are also essential. After a long period when the emphasis of public policy has often been on retirement, it will perhaps not be surprising if employers and older workers are sceptical about the notion of 'active ageing'. It is important, therefore, that policies are long term and consistent in their messages, and are not contradicted by other areas of public policy.

Also, all too frequently, population ageing is discussed in almost apocalyptic terms, but public discussion presented in this way – however well intentioned – may only serve to confirm negative stereotypes. It is perhaps of little surprise that older workers report that they face substantial barriers in the labour market, making them disinclined to seek work, when this negative message is constantly communicated. Even attempts to highlight the positive attributes of older workers run the risk of confirming age stereotypes. Approaches and messages have often been simplistic and ageist.

---

[1] Displacement means that an attendee on a scheme simply displaces someone with whom they compete, ie there is no job creation. Deadweight means that a person moving into a job probably would have done so without the 'help' of a scheme.

Introduction

The policy and research context

Over the last two decades, against a background of the restructuring of many industrialised economies, there has been a marked trend towards a reduction in the length of working life, with a dramatic fall in labour force participation rates among older workers (Kohli et al, 1991). Until recently, policies in many developed economies, particularly in Western Europe, encouraged or facilitated early exit of older workers from the labour market, while labour market policy was almost exclusively aimed at tackling youth unemployment (see for example, Gruber and Wise, 1999). According to Anne-Marie Guillemard (1997), the passage from work to retirement has undergone a profound change in Europe with the "deinstitutionalisation of the threefold model of the life course" (p 443). According to Guillemard, in a number of countries, public retirement systems have been replaced as the primary means of regulating definitive exit from the labour force, while, elsewhere, a significant proportion move in to inactivity via other arrangements (pp 446-7). Disability and unemployment insurance funds have been utilised in particular as alternative pathways to inactivity. Eligibility criteria have been loosened and coverage increased in order to accommodate older workers with limited re-employment prospects. Added to this, pre-retirement schemes have been utilised in order to facilitate the exit of older workers, often as a policy of creating jobs for younger people (pp 448-9). Guillemard states that this "development has led to an increasing number of in-between, usually unstable, statuses between work and retirement" (1997, p 451) and the "'destandardisation' of the life course, as the ages at which people stop working become more and more dispersed" (p 454).

Research also points to the existence of widespread age discrimination in the labour market, with employers seemingly reluctant to recruit, train or retain older workers (Taylor and Walker, 1998).

However, in recent years, with population ageing, concerns about escalating pension costs and declining participation rates, policy makers have begun to explore options for extending working lives. A new consensus is emerging around the notion of active or productive ageing. The European Commission has set out its vision for realising this with the following list of requirements:

- improving the skills, motivation and mobility of older workers;
- good practice in lifelong learning is promoted and disseminated;
- adapting workplaces to workforce ageing, to reduce the erosion of workability and to extend working lives;
- facilitating access to more suitable and flexible forms of working for ageing workers;
- removing age-discriminatory attitudes and practices (EC, 1999, p 5).

Added to this is the view that: "Successful active ageing policies involve all generations. All actors (government, firms and workers) need to adopt life-cycle strategies enabling workers of all ages to stay longer in employment" (EC, 1999, p 5). In his keynote introductory report to the European Commission Conference on Active Ageing, Alan Walker identified the following key themes, among others:

- Active ageing has the potential for major social and economic impact via the development of new, more active and employment/activity-friendly approaches with regard to pensions, employment, health and social care and citizenship.

- Bringing together the different elements of policy is essential if active ageing is to become more than a slogan. A multidimensional strategy will integrate individual and collective action and concentrate attention on the whole of the life course, not only older people.

- Achieving active ageing across the life course requires policy makers to adopt holistic and 'joined-up' approaches (Walker, 1999, p 2).

Similarly, the Organisation for Economic Co-operation and Development (OECD) has set out the following list of reforms that are required in order for active ageing to be achieved:

- Greater emphasis on prevention, making inexpensive interventions such as providing public information at an early stage of life and thereby reducing the need for later remedial action.

- Use of remedial interventions that are less fragmented and which are concentrated at critical transition points in life – early identification of problems, use of case management techniques, coordination among various agencies and measurement of outcomes.

- Better balance in the lifetime costs and benefits of social security programming to provide less constrained choices and greater responsibility at the level of individuals, such as greater linkage of lifetime pension contributions and benefits.

- Without a common strategic framework for reform, changes in one area can offset reforms in another; reforms necessarily cut across traditional programme boundaries. A common framework would also improve the quality of on-the-ground service delivery by facilitating cooperation between many agencies. There would be opportunity for sharing of lessons learned across disciplines and exchange of data and research results (Auer and Fortuny, 1999, p 26).

Many countries are already implementing policies to reduce age discrimination in the labour market, encouraging the recruitment of older workers, delaying retirement, encouraging the sharing of best practice among employers or helping older workers seeking guidance or training. There is increasing debate about how to overcome age

barriers and to extend the working lives of older people, for example, options for more flexible retirement, for the reintegration of older workers and for improving their employability. Increasingly the debate is shifting from one about 'older workers' to 'age diversity' and the life course more generally, and to considering the heterogeneity of 'older workers' when formulating policies.

This study aimed to contribute to current debates by providing a commentary on recent developments in public policies in selected countries and highlighting the lessons these provide for policy makers in the UK.

Methodology

The research consisted of a literature review, coupled with visits to a selected number of countries: Australia, the USA, Finland, Germany, Japan and the Netherlands. These countries were chosen because policy making towards older workers is already quite well advanced or emerging rapidly (for example Japan has a long history of policy making for older workers; see Campbell, 1992; Kimura and Oka, 2001).

Each case study involved interviews with academic experts, policy makers and practitioners to obtain up-to-date information on the situation of older workers in the labour markets of each country and policy making regarding age and employment.

The fieldwork in Finland and Germany took place in July 2001, the USA in September and Japan and Australia in November and December. The fieldwork concluded with a visit to the Netherlands in February 2002.

The advantage of this approach over desk research or telephone interviews was that, in some instances, policies have been implemented relatively recently and it is unlikely that a significant literature has emerged around the initiative. Also, there is value in exploring the process of policy development and implementation in detail, which is better carried out nearer the time of implementation and in face-to-face interviews. Additionally, this approach provided the opportunity to explore the emergence of policy initiatives from multiple perspectives. Finally, new policies are emerging rapidly in these countries, which means that written sources date quickly.

Structure of the report

After this introductory chapter and discussion of the methodology for the research, the report begins with a brief discussion of population ageing and then by an overview of the labour market situation of older workers in the countries studied (Chapter 2). Then, the report considers policy making on age and employment (Chapters 3-7). It describes and compares initiatives, and reports the findings of evaluations and the views of key informants. The report concludes (Chapter 8) with a discussion of implications for public policy and provides an outline framework for the development of policies in this area.

2

Population ageing and older workers in the case study countries

Ageing populations

As a result of declining or stable fertility rates and an increase in life expectancy, the populations of the case study countries are set to age markedly over the next 50 years. Table 1 shows fertility rates and life expectancy at birth in the countries between 1980 and 2000. With the exception of the USA, fertility rates fell between 1980 and 2000, and markedly so in Japan. Japan also has the longest life expectancy at birth. Table 2 reports the proportion of the population of the case study countries between 1980 and 2050 aged over 60 and 65. This shows that their populations are set to age markedly over the next 50 years. Japan will have the most aged population, with over a third of its population being over age 60 or 65 by 2050. In contrast, the USA will be the least aged, with just over a quarter and fifth of its population being over age 60 or 65 by 2050.

Table 1: Fertility rates and life expectancy

| | Fertility rates | | Life expectancy | | | |
	1980-1985	1995-2000	1980-1985	1995-2000	1980-1985	1995-2000
Australia	1.9	1.8	71.9	75.5	78.7	81.1
Finland	1.7	1.7	70.0	73.0	77.9	80.6
Germany	1.5	1.3	70.3	73.9	76.8	80.2
Japan	1.8	1.4	74.2	76.8	79.7	82.9
Netherlands	1.5	1.5	72.8	75.0	79.4	80.7
UK	1.8	1.7	71.0	74.5	77.2	79.8
USA	1.8	2.0	70.9	73.4	78.3	80.1

Source: World Labour Report (ILO, 2000)

Table 2: Population aged over 60 and 65

| | Population over 60 (% total population) | | | | | Population over 65 (% total population) | | | | |
	1980	2000	2010	2030	2050	1980	2000	2010	2030	2050
Australia	13.7	16.2	19.2	26.1	28.4	9.6	12.1	13.4	20.0	22.6
Finland	16.4	19.9	24.6	31.6	31.6	12.0	14.9	17.0	25.3	25.6
Germany	19.3	23.2	25.3	34.4	35.3	15.6	16.4	19.8	26.1	28.4
Japan	12.9	23.1	29.3	34.2	37.6	9.0	17.1	21.5	27.3	31.8
Netherlands	15.7	18.4	22.6	33.4	34.5	11.5	13.8	15.8	25.6	28.1
UK	20.1	21.0	23.5	30.0	31.3	15.1	16.0	17.1	23.1	24.9
USA	15.6	16.4	18.7	26.4	27.8	11.2	12.5	13.2	20.6	21.7

Source: World Labour Report (ILO, 2000)

The labour market and older workers

This section discusses trends in labour force participation, employment and unemployment rates. Table 3 shows trends in labour force participation among older men and women between 1979 and 2000. For the purpose of comparison, UK figures are also presented. This shows that, since 1979, in Australia and the European countries, there has been a marked decline in labour force participation rates among older men. While there has been a downward trend in the USA also, this has been less marked. In Japan there has been a slight decline from a high level. Overall, in terms of older male participation rates, the European case study countries are some way behind Australia, the USA and the UK, and all are a considerable way behind Japan. There is evidence that this decline in participation has reversed, and markedly so in the European case countries, but not the USA and the UK where this increase has been slight. By contrast, rates in Japan have remained fairly stable.

Table 3 shows that labour force participation among older women is increasing. However, as with men it also shows that the participation of older women in the European countries is some way behind that of Japan and the USA, although catching up.

The increase in female participation rates can be attributed to the increasing propensity of successive age cohorts of women to work. Thus, the ageing labour force will increasingly be a female one. In future this may present policy makers and employers with a number of challenges, as it is argued that "women may have

employment goals, career patterns, and work styles different from their male counterparts" (Hansson et al, 1997, p 221). Policy makers and employers will need to consider the training needs of older women, the likelihood that they will have caring responsibilities, and that they may have different orientations to work and retirement (Hansson et al, 1997, pp 222-3).

However, it should be noted that early retirement has been both a male and a female phenomenon. For example, between 1960 and 1995 the average retirement age of men and women in Australia fell by approximately four and five years respectively, and approximately one year in Japan for both men and women (Klös, undated; Auer and Fortuny, 1999, p 11).

The decline in labour force participation among those aged 50 and over has been attributed to a number of economic, political and social factors. Older men have tended to be over-represented in declining industries and under-represented in industries experiencing growth, and are thus affected by a reduced demand for unskilled workers (Trinder, 1989; Jacobs et al, 1991). During periods of economic expansion and contraction, when labour demands have grown and receded respectively, the labour force participation of older men has fluctuated accordingly. As employers cut back on recruitment, it is younger workers who are predominantly affected (Lindley et al, 1991); however, if an employer needs to shed staff, it is older workers who are affected disproportionately (Leppel and Heller Clain, 1995). During recessions, older workers have been utilised in early exit strategies to counter problems with youth unemployment (Trinder, 1989; Kohli et al, 1991). Early retirement has

Table 3: Labour force participation rates among men and women aged 55-64 between 1979 and 2000

	Men					Women				
	1979	1983	1990	1995	2000	1979	1983	1990	1995	2000
Australia	69.5	62.0	63.2	60.8	61.5	20.3	20.5	24.9	28.6	36.3
Finland	56.3	54.1	47.1	41.6	48.1	41.3	47.4	40.8	42.9	45.2
Germany	66.9	63.1	58.3	52.7	55.2	28.4	26.3	27.5	28.1	34.1
Netherlands	65.3	54.2	45.7	41.4	50.8	14.4	14.4	16.7	18.6	26.4
UK	–	71.5	68.1	62.4	63.3	–	–	38.7	40.8	42.6
EU	–	–	56.6	51.5	53.0	–	–	26.5	27.0	31.0
Japan	85.2	84.7	83.3	84.8	84.1	45.4	46.1	47.2	48.5	49.7
USA	72.8	69.4	67.8	66.0	67.3	41.7	41.5	45.2	49.2	51.8

Source: OECD *Employment outlook* (various)

become an important feature of labour market dynamics, as increased prosperity and burgeoning leisure opportunities together with the growth of occupational pensions has encouraged a proportion of those who can afford to, to retire. At the same time, age barriers in internal and external labour markets have limited older workers' employment prospects.

It might be asked why labour force participation among Japanese older workers has been consistently higher than that among older workers in other countries. Several possible factors have been identified:

- A high proportion of self-employed or 'family workers' for whom receipt of a pension has not been dependent on retirement.
- In certain sectors and in micro-businesses, until the late 1980s workers could claim a full pension after the age of 60 while receiving full-time wages.
- Part-time employment while claiming a partial pension.
- Among former civil servants it has been possible to receive a full pension and draw a salary while working in second jobs in the private sector, although this option was ended by the mid-1990s.
- Low pension replacement rates.
- Improving health among older people (Koshiro, 1996, pp 102, 104).

Older workers' employment

Table 4 shows trends in employment/population ratios between 1979 and 2000 among men and women aged 55-64. Australia, Finland and the Netherlands have experienced sharp increases in male employment/population ratios between 1995 and 2000, albeit to levels far below those observed in 1979. Similarly, Australia, Finland and the Netherlands have experienced marked increases in female employment/population ratios since 1995. In the USA and the UK increases have been less dramatic, and in Japan there was a slight decrease from 1995 to 2000 among older men while the picture for women was static.

Higher educational attainment is associated with a lower risk of unemployment among older workers. Tables 5 and 6 show this to be the case for each of the countries for which data was available. Workers with only secondary levels of education tend to experience much higher rates of unemployment than those with a tertiary level of education.

Table 4: Employment/population ratios among men and women aged 55-64 between 1979 and 2000

| | Men | | | | | Women | | | | |
	1979	1983	1990	1995	2000	1979	1983	1990	1995	2000
Australia	67.4	59.6	59.2	55.3	61.5	19.8	19.9	24.2	27.4	35.4
Finland	54.3	51.4	46.3	34.9	43.7	39.0	44.1	39.7	33.1	40.9
Germany	63.2	57.4	52.0	47.2	48.2	26.8	24.0	22.4	24.4	29.0
Netherlands	63.2	46.1	44.5	39.9	49.9	14.0	13.2	15.8	18.0	25.8
UK	–	64.3	62.4	56.1	59.8	–	–	36.7	39.3	41.4
EU	–	–	53.1	47.2	48.9	–	–	24.7	24.9	28.4
Japan	81.5	80.5	80.4	80.8	78.4	44.8	45.1	46.5	47.5	47.8
USA	70.8	65.2	65.2	63.6	65.6	40.4	39.4	44.0	47.5	50.5

Source: OECD *Employment outlook* (various)

Table 5: Unemployment and educational attainment among older workers aged 45-54

	Australia		Finland		Germany		Japan		Netherlands		UK		USA	
	M	W	M	W	M	W	M	W	M	W	M	W	M	W
Pre-primary and primary					4.5	2.5							–	–
Lower secondary level	43.9	61.4	41.3	43.2	19.7	23.4	27.6	23.8			28.6	27.5	–	–
Upper secondary, general	22.6	14.0	42.2	41.3			51.7	57.1			13.2	–	49.9	–
Upper secondary, vocational or technical, long											23.3	12.6		
Upper secondary, vocational or technical, short											20.2	28.9		
Tertiary university	12.3	9.0	–	–	8.8	7.2	17.2	4.8			11.0	12.2	–	
Tertiary non-university	10.6	12.5	10.0*	10.2*	7.9	6.9	3.4	14.3			–	–	–	–

M=men, W=women

* Figures should be treated with caution (cell sizes are small making data unreliable)

– Data too unreliable

Figures unavailable for the Netherlands

Source: OECD Labour Force Statistics database

Table 6: Unemployment and educational attainment among older workers aged 55-64

	Australia		Finland		Germany		Japan		Netherlands		UK		USA	
	M	W	M	W	M	W	M	W	M	W	M	W	M	W
Pre-primary and primary					2.9								–	–
Lower secondary level	44.3	61.3	47.9	54.3	17.5	26.6	37.5	50.0			28.0	35.3	–	–
Upper secondary, general	25.1	15.5	32.5*	29.3*			45.8	42.9			11.7	–	52.0	64.8
Upper secondary, vocational or technical, long											25.3	–		
Upper secondary, vocational or technical, short											14.9	37.1		
Tertiary university	11.1	4.0	–	–	11.1	3.3	14.6				12.5	–	–	–
Tertiary non-university	9.4	18.0	–	–	11.1	8.7	2.1	7.1			–	–	–	–

M=men, W=women

* Figures should be treated with caution (cell sizes are small making data unreliable)

– Data too unreliable

Figures unavailable for the Netherlands

Unemployment and long-term unemployment

Table 7 presents unemployment rates among men and women aged 55-64 between 1979 and 2000. Particularly notable is the remarkable increase in both male and female unemployment rates in the mid-1990s in several countries (particularly in Finland), which, while declining in recent years, have yet to return to previous levels. Also notable are high levels of unemployment among men, and in particular women in Germany. It is also notable that, while low compared to some European countries, unemployment rates for

older men and women in Japan increased markedly between 1995 and 2000.

Table 8 shows that long-term unemployment in the year 2000 was significantly higher among those aged 55 or over than in other age groups. This is a particular problem for men and women in Germany, where over two thirds of the unemployed in this age group were long-term unemployed. The incidence of male long-term unemployment was lower in Japan than Australia and the European countries, while the UK had the lowest incidence of female long-term unemployment, followed by Japan.

Table 7: Unemployment rates among men and women aged 55-64 between 1979 and 2000

| | Men | | | | | Women | | | | |
	1979	1983	1990	1995	2000	1979	1983	1990	1995	2000
Australia	3.1	3.8	6.3	9.0	4.9	2.3	2.9	3.0	4.0	2.4
Finland	3.6	5.1	1.8	16.3	9.3	5.5	7.0	2.8	22.8	9.4
Germany	5.5	9.0	9.9	10.4	12.6	5.9	8.6	15.2	13.1	15.0
Netherlands	3.3	14.9	2.8	3.6	1.7	2.7	8.2	6.3	3.2	2.1
UK	–	10.1	8.4	10.1	5.5	–	–	5.0	3.7	2.8
EU	–	–	6.2	8.4	7.8	–	–	6.9	7.6	8.3
Japan	4.4	5.0	3.4	4.7	6.8	1.2	2.1	1.4	2.1	3.6
USA	2.7	6.1	3.8	3.6	2.4	3.2	5.0	2.8	3.6	2.5

Source: OECD *Employment outlook* (various)

Table 8: Incidence of long-term unemployment in 2000 among men and women in different age groups (% of unemployed)

| | Men | | | Women | | |
	15-24	25-54	55 plus	15-24	25-54	55 plus
Australia	17.8	36.6	45.5	16.0	28.3	56.0
Finland	8.8*	39.1	58.3	8.8*	29.6	54.5
Germany	23.7	49.1	69.1	23.2	52.9	69.1
Japan	26.3	29.4	35.6	14.8	13.8	37.5
Netherlands	–	35.5	56.9	12.5*	38.6	43.9*
UK	17.4	40.3	46.1	9.9	22.9	30.5
USA	–	6.8	–	–	6.4	–

* Figures should be treated with caution (cell sizes are small making data unreliable)
– Data too unreliable
Source: OECD Labour Force Statistics database

3

Public policies for older workers

Among the countries studied there is an increasing emphasis on extending working life. There have been several drivers of this:

- demographic change;
- financing of public pension systems;
- a shift of responsibility for pension coverage to the individual;
- a shift of responsibility for the cost of early retirement to the worker or firm;
- skills and labour shortages;
- early retirement schemes provided few job opportunities for younger workers;
- a general shift from passive to active employment policies;
- a belief that employment problems should be tackled directly rather than offloaded on to the state;
- a growing recognition of the problem of age discrimination in the labour market;
- in Japan and to an extent in Finland, not having a history of immigration has encouraged a greater emphasis on retaining older workers.

At the same time, there are factors working against the reintegration of older workers, such as relatively high levels of unemployment, high levels of work intensity and an early exit culture in some countries resulting in pressure for early retirement.

In recent years there has been a marked shift away from passive to active labour market programmes in many countries. Much of the decline in passive spending can be accounted for by a decline in early retirement schemes since the mid-1980s (OECD, 2001, p 28). Governments are keen to increase the supply of older workers and to stimulate demand by lowering the costs of employing them and are thus removing incentives

for early retirement, increasing the age of access to state pensions and introducing incentives to remain in the labour force. Flexibilisation of retirement is also being attempted, with gradual retirement possible in some countries. Some countries have also implemented active labour market programmes targeting older workers. Employment subsidy schemes have been commonly implemented, while schemes offering vocational guidance and training have been somewhat less common. Some governments have also implemented awareness-raising campaigns among employers and the general public. However, the wish of policy makers to extend work life often appears to be at odds with the desire of employers, trades unions and older workers themselves for early retirement. Policies are summarised in Table 9.

What this table does not show well is the extent to which policies are developed in particular countries. While this is a somewhat subjective assessment it would appear that policy making is most developed in the areas of pension and social security reform and less developed in the area of employment policy. A detailed discussion is provided below and in the following chapters.

Integrated and strategic policy approaches

Much has been made recently of the need for an integrated life course approach to public policy on age and employment. However, with the particular exception of Finland, the picture is generally one of piecemeal and ad hoc policy making on this issue, although attempts are now underway to take a more strategic approach (for example in Australia, Japan and the Netherlands),

Table 9: Main public policies affecting older workers among the countries studied

Comprehensive/strategic policy approach to the employment and retirement of older workers	Australia, Finland, Japan
Removing incentives to early retirement and encouraging later retirement	Australia, Finland, Germany, Japan, Netherlands, USA
Abolition of mandatory retirement	Australia, USA
Gradual retirement schemes	Finland, Germany, Netherlands
Age discrimination legislation, protection against dismissal, proscription of age bars in recruitment advertisements	Australia, Finland, Germany, Japan, USA
Awareness raising campaigns among employers and the general public	Australia, Finland, Germany, Netherlands
Guidance and training programmes targeting older workers	Australia, Finland, Germany, Japan, Netherlands, USA
Support to employers eg advice and guidance, training, employment placements	Australia, Finland, Germany, Japan, USA
Support to labour market intermediaries	Germany, USA
Employment subsidy and other employment incentive schemes	Australia, Finland, Germany, Japan, Netherlands

although this is at a very early stage. This section discusses integrated and strategic approaches in the case countries.

The drivers of Finland's Programme on Ageing Workers (1998-2002) were concerns about population ageing and the fact that the labour force participation of people aged over 60 was lower in Finland than the European average. The Ministry of Social Affairs and Health had overall responsibility for the programme, with the Ministry of Labour and the Ministry of Education the other lead departments. Other national government departments were involved, as were the Association of Finnish Local Authorities, the Social Insurance Institution, the Institute of Occupational Health and pensions companies. The programme involved 40 projects targeting those aged 45 and over, which were divided between the ministries.

In the Finnish Ministry of Social Affairs and Health some of the projects were concerned with occupational health services and occupational safety and health activities, in particular in small- and medium-sized enterprises. The programme included information campaigns, as well as training to stimulate activities related to the maintenance and improved working capacity of older workers. Information and training was directed at occupational health service personnel,

labour and trade centres, staff at employment offices, employers and workers themselves.

An integral part of the programme was extensive research and development activities, and a databank was compiled to make information available to enterprises to use in developing their own projects. Systems were also developed for occupational health services and occupational safety and employment authorities, to help them to monitor and utilise the research and development activities related to maintaining working capacity.

Another aim of the programme was to raise awareness of Finland's part-time pension scheme. From 1998 it has been possible to retire on a part-time pension at age 56, instead of 58 as previously, with employers obliged to offer part-time work to those who wish to do so (Sorsa, 1999). The programme also involved exploring options to reduce the usage of early retirement pathways.

Various measures to improve the situation of older jobseekers were the responsibility of the Ministry of Labour. The most important of these was to diversify and develop the employment service to make its services suitable for older workers. Attempts have therefore been made to tailor services such as rehabilitation and training.

Other objectives were to increase the share of older people in employment-promoting adult education and among those employed via employment subsidies. Another focus of the programme was encouraging companies to pay more attention to older employees in terms of training and to develop options for flexible employment. Promoting better intergenerational relations in employment was another activity.

Communication and awareness raising was a key part of the programme. As part of this, the Ministry of Labour, in cooperation with labour market organisations, organised an awareness raising campaign for employers, aimed to change attitudes towards older workers.

The Ministry of Education had responsibility for 10 of the 40 objectives of the programme. The aim was to develop adult education so that it would better meet the needs of the population aged 45 and over. This included the expert seminar 'Age and learning' in 1998. Converting the principle of lifelong learning into practical solutions was another objective. Proposals for a national strategy for life-long learning were developed. An important target group for the programme was teachers – one third of whom are aged over 50. Supporting their skills maintenance and coping with working life were central objectives of the programme.

However, the Programme on Ageing Workers has been criticised for being too top down and government led, with insufficient support for grassroots activities. Respondents in this research felt that too little attention had been paid to reintegrating the unemployed compared to attempts to retain older workers in employment. In the view of one respondent, despite the programme and despite economic growth in Finland, the prospects for unemployed older workers have not improved much[2]. Another view was that more work needed to be undertaken at the level of individual firms, in addition to costly media campaigns. It was also felt that the Ministry of Education had not participated fully in the programme.

It is also important to consider that Finland's population size perhaps makes an integrated

national policy of this kind easier to achieve. In the USA, for example, it was felt that integration like that achieved in Finland would be almost impossible, given the structure of American governance. Instead, it was argued, the push was towards *dis*integration in policy making. Also, it was felt that attempts at integration have resulted in battles between special interest groups to retain their leverage within government. Segmented lobby interests have prevented holistic approaches.

The USA does not have a national coordinated policy on age or older workers. However, the Federal Department of Health and Human Services and the Archstone Foundation have established an expert committee to examine trends in the ageing of the workforce and to identify the range of policy and research issues that should be addressed. States have also addressed this issue individually. For example, in 1995 the Governor of North Carolina appointed an older workers' expert taskforce.

When considering the integration of public policy it is also important to consider the fit between policies on age and employment with other policies. In this regard it would appear that policy making is also not particularly nuanced in the countries studied. Also, the promotion of 'age diversity' as opposed to the narrower concept of 'older workers' is not much developed.

An Australian model, which might have applicability at the regional level in the UK, is the state government of Queensland's Breaking the Unemployment Cycle initiative. Launched in 1998, this is a 'whole of government' employment initiative the central aim of which is reducing Queensland's rate of unemployment to 5% within five years. This is outlined in Box 1. However, it should be noted that in Australia as a whole a more integrated approach is only just emerging. Some states have had policies on 'mature age' employment for some time, ostensibly in order to fill gaps in Commonwealth provision. However, the Commonwealth government has just begun to develop a comprehensive strategy on the employment of older workers, while social welfare reforms are already being implemented. It does not appear that state and federal policy making has been particularly integrated so far.

---

[2] In fact, as shown above, unemployment rates among older workers in Finland have declined somewhat in recent years, although they remain relatively high.

Box 1: Breaking the unemployment cycle (Queensland, Australia)

On coming into office in June 1998, the Queensland government established a major employment initiative with the principal objective of bringing unemployment in Queensland down to 5% within five years. The Jobs Policy Council (JPC) was set up as a peak policy council and comprised the Minister for Employment, Training and Industrial Relations and the Chief Executive Officers of all relevant government departments. It oversees the Breaking the Unemployment Cycle initiatives and identifies future employment creation opportunities. The JPC reports to the special purpose cabinet committee on employment, which is responsible for setting the broad strategic direction for government-wide employment initiatives. The JPC also consults with the Youth Jobs Taskforce (Premiers Department) and other employment creation programmes to ensure that there is a comprehensive, government-wide approach to employment creation.

In February 1999, the Employment Taskforce of the Department of Employment, Training and Industrial Relations (DETIR), working with the Healthy Ageing Research Unit of the University of Queensland, submitted research findings detailing the current and potential issues flowing from mature age (over 45) employment and unemployment to the JPC. The Council endorsed recommendations for a programme of concerted government and community actio to combat mature age unemployment.

The Breaking the Unemployment Cycle initiative, administered by the Employment Taskforce of the DETIR, addresses unemployment as a whole (including mature aged unemployment) and has adopted a joined-up government-wide approach to strategic policy and action directions.

Community Employment Assistance Program

Through the Community Employment Assistance Program (CEAP), the DETIR funds community organisations to provide job search, placement and vocational training assistance to individuals who are long-term unemployed. Mid-August 1999, nine organisations had received grants for projects that specifically assisted mature age unemployed people, while many other projects included mature age people within their target groups.

One example is the Cairns Employment Services for Mature Aged, which incorporates a combination of intensive job searching activities, work experience and direct canvassing of employers for mature age jobseekers from 35 to 60 years old. The project supervisor is also involved in directly marketing mature age employment to employers, to increase the organisation's employer database and the chances of sustainable employment.

Community Jobs Plan

The Community Jobs Plan is a government initiative which funds job placement opportunities in community organisations, local councils and statutory authorities of three to six months' duration, for people who are long-term unemployed. Mid-August 1999, four organisations had received grants for projects designed to provide employment opportunities for disadvantaged mature age jobseekers from culturally diverse backgrounds. One of these projects is the Gladstone Mosquito Survey and Eradication Project in which participants undertake complete door-to-door (9,500) inspections of the city, provide advice on mosquito management, identify and survey breeding sites and carry out preventative action. The project aims to employ as inspectors mature age long-term unemployed people.

Regional forums

Through Regional Forums, the Queensland government has seized the opportunity to take a leadership role in the development of appropriate policies and strategies to address, not only unemployment as a whole, but mature age unemployment.

Representatives of the JPC have undertaken visits throughout Queensland, particularly in unemployment blackspots and areas with high levels of skills shortages. The Commissioner for Training and a number of Members of the Legislative Assembly hosted the forums, which were attended by representatives from business, unions, employers' organisations, community organisations, training providers, schools, local councils and government. Responses and strategies to address the issues raised at the forums are now being considered through consultations led by the DETIR with other Queensland government departments.

Employment brokerage response teams

The response teams have been established to provide an immediate service to redundant workers from communities facing major social and economic dislocation. The process involves supporting redundant workers through an interview in which future employment and training options are discussed. Information is also provided on other areas of support such as financial assistance.

Worker Assistance Program

The Worker Assistance Program is an early intervention labour market programme that assists workers displaced as a result of large-scale redundancies in making the transition to alternative employment. The programme acts as a circuit breaker, to help prevent displaced workers from becoming long-term unemployed and reduce the likelihood of considerable detriment to local communities resulting from substantial job losses.

Although all eligible workers are given the same level of service and consideration, the primary target group are those assessed by the immediate response teams as being at risk of becoming long-term unemployed. This group includes eligible workers who are aged 45 and over, disabled people, those from non-English speaking backgrounds, indigenous Australians, people lacking literacy and numeracy skills and low-skilled workers.

Jobs Policy Council Mature Age Employment and Unemployment Initiative

The Council has authorised a major initiative (to be coordinated by the DETIR) to address the issue of mature age employment and unemployment in Queensland. The initiative involves research and implementation of strategies to address the following:

1. Existing barriers to mature age employment in the areas of:

- job recruitment, retirement, early retirement, and redundancy and exit;
- training, development and promotion;
- flexible working practice, including part time;
- ergonomics and job design.

Research will also focus on processes to bring about change in managers' and workers' attitudes to older workers possibly involving an Action Research methodology where the effect of interventions in human resource management is evaluated, the findings serving as a basis for policy development. Overseas experience in combating age barriers including successful employer initiatives that have positive bottom-line consequences while increasing retention and recruitment levels for older workers will be shared in workshops and featured in the information kit.

2. A number of Queensland businesses will cooperate in developing strategies to inform employers of the business benefits to employers of retaining/retraining mature age employees, such as:

- accurately determining magnitude of turnover costs to support the value of retaining/retraining older workers;
- using to advantage the responsiveness of mature age employees to mature age clients;
- avoiding loss of corporate memory through work-to-retirement transition;
- benefiting from the experience and mentoring capacity of older workers.

3. Researching best practice models in leading Queensland organisations in the facilitation of recruitment and retention of older workers. This may involve an Action Research methodology where the effect of an intervention in human resource management practice is evaluated, the findings serving as the basis for policy development.

4. Conducting a major education and awareness raising programme for employers, managers and the community including:

- a major workforce symposium 'Experience pays', which was conducted in August 1999 for 150 participants;
- the development of an information kit to assist employers to understand the value of having older workers, to manage the older workforce effectively and to assist employees in preparing for the new knowledge economy;
- a series of regional workshops designed to inform employers and the community about the mature aged workforce and the value of experience and to commence a process of collaborative strategy development.

5. The development of systemic policies to allow the public service to lead by example in the employment of older workers.

6. The development of supportive infrastructures where necessary.

7. A joined-up approach to resolving the issues.

Queensland Department of Main Roads

The Queensland Department of Main Roads has begun researching and implementing strategies to address the challenges presented by its mature age workers. Over 50% of the department's workers are aged 40 and over, and the proportion is growing. The risk of significant loss of experience and corporate memory as these people approach the age of retirement has been acknowledged and the department's Workforce Capability Unit has therefore developed a Mature Age Worker Project to develop options and choices for their mature age workers based on mutual benefit. Options may include flexible working arrangements, mentoring and work shadowing to create a different type of work relationship and allowing a greater range of lifestyle choices.

Queensland Office of The Public Service (OPS)

The OPS is also commencing a major project to address the problem of loss of intellectual capital due to large numbers of retiring employees across the Queensland Public Service (19.27% are over 50 and 8.3% are over 55). The project provides recommendations on strategies to reduce barriers to mature age employment. It will also investigate potential effects on agency performance, and the implications for employee entitlements, part-time employment, taxation, superannuation, leave and possible legislative and employee relations issues. A seminar on successful mentoring conducted for the Queensland Public Service by OPS will further promote continuity of corporate knowledge and formally valuing the contribution of older workers.

The OPS, with the Employment Taskforce (DETIR), is steering the development of strategies which will allow the Queensland Public Service to 'lead by example' in its employment practices with respect to the mature age employee, as initiated by the JPC.

Office of Ageing, Department of Families, Youth and Community Care

The Office of Ageing is developing the Queensland Framework for Ageing 2000-04, which incorporates employment and retirement planning issues as one of the four key areas for action. Community consultation meetings, which included the issue of employment and mature age workers were held throughout the state. The Office of Ageing in conjunction with the Anti-Discrimination Commission Queensland (ADCQ) jointly conducted a phone-in on age discrimination during 1998. The majority of callers (76%) telephoned in relation to alleged incidents of age discrimination in the area of employment.

Establishing a business

The Department of State Development provides a range of programmes aimed at improving business diversity, prosperity and economic growth. The Office of Small Business has responsibility for the development and coordination of services aimed specifically at small business and people wishing to set up a business. Given the size of the intended market and the relatively long incubation period between when a client has a business idea and when the actually start up their own business, the department refrains from providing high levels of personalised advice. While there is no focus on assisting mature age people to start up a business, anecdotal reports indicate that the majority of clients are over 40.

The Anti-Discrimination Commission Queensland (ADCQ)

The Commission has a statutory duty to raise community awareness about discrimination issues. It conducts an average of four education/training sessions per week in roughly equal proportions across the public, private and community sectors throughout Queensland. All sessions include reference to age discrimination. The Commission has published a brochure entitled 'Age discrimination – your rights and responsibilities.'

Vocational Education Training and Employment Commission (VETEC)

The Division of Training has developed a wide range of programmes to facilitate access to training for all age groups. The Division is committed to the progressive expansion of quality vocational education and training programmes, to enhance the career and employment opportunities for young people and mature age people to develop a skilled and competitive workforce.

A VET qualification can be achieved via a number of pathways.

Structured training

Apprenticeships and traineeships provide formal learning through work-based training with contractual arrangements between the employee and employer. Over the last few years, the number of people aged over 25 entering apprenticeships and traineeships has increased in line with increasing demand for higher levels of skills in the workforce. A significant proportion of older trainees is already employed (20%). To a large extent the take up of apprenticeships and traineeships by older workers is because of a perception that they provide the only way for their skills to be recognised.

A recent review of the quality and effectiveness of the training system in Queensland pointed to the urgent need for more appropriate responses to existing workers, particularly in gaining new skills and retraining, as well as having their competencies formally recognised. While apprenticeships and traineeships will focus on new labour entrants and people under the age of 24, new options for older people will be developed to ensure their continued employment readiness.

VET qualifications can also be gained through courses at technical and further education institutes, through tendered courses conducted by private providers, and colleges and community organisations. The informal nature of community venues and the additional support provided in a community setting tend to make this a popular option for women, particularly those who face other forms of disadvantage, to gain qualifications.

Access courses

These are generally non-award courses, many of which focus on personal development. Many individuals underestimate their basic educational skills and skills gained through previous work or raising families, and prefer to consolidate these skills prior to entry to formal training.

English language, literacy and numeracy classes

These basic skills classes are very important for people who have not had consistent schooling. This may include people with a disability, Aboriginal and Torres Strait Islander people and people from minority ethnic communities. English language skills are often a major issue in attempting to gain employment.

Access to Employment Outcomes

This programme is for anyone out of the workforce for over six months, and includes, for example, those who have been engaged in caring, in home duties, assisted in running a two-person family business or have been out of work due to illness. It enables spouses who are not eligible for unemployment benefits to retrain. Courses include job skills, workplace information and personal development.

Specific programmes

Programs for People with a Disability are flexible and provide appropriate support services for the participant, while ensuring the integrity and outcomes of the training provided. These programmes span a range of vocations and include pre-vocational courses. Individuals accessing these programmes vary from those with high support needs to those recovering from a long-term illness needing skills to re-enter the workforce.

Women Re-entering the Workforce is contracted by the Open Learning Network to provide training for up to 400 women in rural areas. The training includes basic workplace skills, understanding of workplaces, small business and computer skills.

Aboriginal Torres Strait Islander Programs are offered across a range of industries and to young and mature age workers to gain skills for employment. These programmes are specifically designed and flexibly delivered to suit the needs and cultural differences of the communities.

In Japan the Ministry of Health, Labour and Welfare's (MHLW) current policy package for the employment of older people has three main pillars. The first aims to encourage firms to extend employment up to age 65 by means of various grants. The second includes measures to improve the employment prospects of older workers by strengthening the government's employment services and measures for the promotion of re-employment assistance by employers. The third pillar consists of advisory services and job programmes such as those provided by the Associations of Employment Development for Senior Citizens (AEDSC) and Silver Human Resource Centres (SHRC). This latter aspect of Japanese public policy will be discussed in greater detail later in the report (see Chapter 6).

The MHLW has recently established an Expert Council on Achieving a Society in Which People Can Work Regardless of Age, which consists of experts and representatives of employers and labour unions. It planned to spend 2001 and 2002 examining the issue before putting forward recommendations. Indeed, it has been argued that, because of Japan's rapidly ageing population, it "needs, even more than other countries, to take the initiative in pursuing such efforts" (Iwata, 2002, p 15). Also, Japan has established a Department of Employment Measures for the Elderly and Persons with Disabilities, which aims to promote 'active aging'.

However, in Japan there appears to be some tension between the need for large corporations in some sectors to downsize and public policy making aimed at extending working life.

Research by the MHLW found an increase between 1994 and 2000 in the use of voluntary retirement or dismissals by firms. This was particularly the case in those firms with over 1,000 employees, where its use was reported by 23.8% of firms compared with 8.5% in a previous survey (*Japan Labour Bulletin*, 2001a).

Elsewhere policy making is moving at different speeds both between and within countries. In Germany, for example, the issue of older worker employment is only just coming onto the policy agenda, and it was pointed out that, while there were integrated programmes on youth unemployment bringing together the federal employment agency and regional government, no such integrated policy making was as yet taking place for older workers. Different ministries were active on age issues but working independently of each other.

In the Netherlands, pensions reform has been underway for some time, but discussion of employment policy is only just emerging in the form of the government sponsored Taskforce on Ageing Workers. Its membership includes representatives of the trades unions, employer associations, the personnel profession, academics and the media. An important element of the taskforce's role is to coordinate action on age and employment by academia, trades unions and in the area of the allocation of funds for education, with a particular emphasis on life-long learning. A key area will be the representation of older people and ageing by the media. Another important activity is stimulating action at the regional and local levels. For a more detailed description of its aims and objectives see Box 2. It should be noted that informants did not consider that policy making towards older workers was fully integrated in the Netherlands. For example, there was a view that a current debate concerning disability benefits was proceeding without consideration of ageing, despite the fact that the majority of claimants are older people.

Box 2: Task Force Ouderen en Arbeid (the Netherlands)

The Taskforce Ouderen en Arbeid (Over-Fifties at Work Taskforce) is based on the principle of the active involvement of older people in the labour market. It is funded by the Ministry of Social Affairs and Employment (SZW). It aims to bring about a change of attitude among employers and employees, secure supporting policy from government bodies and provide ready access to information and funding for all those involved. It does this through:

- collection, analysis and dissemination of good practice;
- providing information and advice for employers and employees;
- incentive schemes for projects intended to improve the employment prospects of people aged over 50.

The target group is the whole of society and the full range of communication media are used to provoke debate and provide follow-up information:

- the bulletin 'Langer' (Longer) reports on developments and opinions;
- the website (www.ouderenenarbeid.nl) gives an overview of the taskforce's goals, progress made and the history of the taskforce – the structure of the website allows easy access to information;
- the database 'Goed gedaan' (Well done) provides information on Dutch and European examples of good practice;
- the brochure series 'Beeldenstorm' (Reform) confronts attitudes with innovative approaches.

The taskforce believes that acceptance by all generations is necessary for success. This involves:

- positive definitions of older, elderly or senior;
- building on the report of the Policy Research Council – *Generatiebewust beleid* (Generation-aware policy);
- tailoring careers to individual desires and capabilities;
- taking into account aspects such as life-long learning, carer roles and daily routines.

The taskforce's aim is for older people to no longer be the 'underdogs' of the labour market. It hopes to achieve this by promoting age-aware personnel and labour market policies, which encompass all ages and therefore are suitable for everyone. Individual capabilities rather than age should be used as the yardstick, although capabilities will change with age.

Myth busting

The taskforce will undertake a knowledge offensive, commencing with a systematic review of current research on older people and the labour market. This will be subjected to analysis and publicity. Furthermore, the taskforce acts as an industry consultant to decision makers, personnel officers and management to help improve their policies and practices relating to the ageing of the population. The taskforce promotes relevant research as well as undertaking and publishing research. Reports on the following will be published:

- trends in the levels of participation in the labour force by older people;
- opinions held by the different generations, employers, employees and jobseekers;
- company culture with respect to age;
- commercial approaches to investing in different age groups;
- entrepreneurship among older people: 'mature beginners';
- older people and the media;
- good practice examples.

From the outset, the taskforce has taken advice from recognised experts in the field. During the first few months of its existence, a conference of interested academics was organised to identify and illuminate current thinking, views, dilemmas and gaps, by building on the findings of national and international research.

The battle against exclusion

The task force wishes to build on the initiatives of the European Commission, which is trying to transfer the positive results it has obtained in the fight against discrimination on the grounds of gender or ethnic background to other areas of discrimination. The taskforce views age discrimination as often going hand in hand with other types of disadvantage, such as gender, disability or race. Added to this, matters related to age do not affect all groups in the population in the same way. The taskforce aims to promote synergy between non-discrimination movements, through supporting new and existing projects, such as:

- non-discrimination and equal treatment in relation to age;
- connection with other types of discrimination under the heading of 'diversity';
- understanding stereotyping and stigmatisation in the workplace;
- introducing a code of practice;
- working to change the image of older people in the media.

The taskforce wants employers to make better use of the knowledge, experience and other qualities that mature people offer. It regards the under-representation of older people as a serious handicap in trade and industry and in the media. The taskforce therefore promotes activities and projects aimed at:

- encouraging young and old to work together within companies;
- improving visibility of temporary workers aged over 65 and older people starting new businesses;
- encouraging older people to mentor young employees;
- praising or vilifying the image of the people aged over 55, as presented in the media.

The battle for greater public acceptance

The taskforce is entering into an ongoing dialogue with political and civic organisations at national, regional and local levels. These include organisations with members of all types: employers, employees, older people, young people, women and minority ethnic groups as well as professional organisations in the areas of personnel management and the labour market, working conditions, labour market mediation, non-discrimination, education, culture and the media. Through this it hopes to promote lively debate via:

- exchange meetings, expert meetings and work visits;
- a 'stay in work' 'phone line for people to receive advice and resolve complaints.

The battle against a future with no prospects

Economic factors may well be an incentive for encouraging older people to work for longer. However, the taskforce has opted for a broader approach, which offers older people a more positive future of full and continuing development, social involvement and the mobilisation of positive energy. An element of this is promoting measures that anticipate the capabilities and limitations of older people. This could range from regular job swapping in order to avoid monotony or stress, to the realisation of an ambition or a re-evaluation of one's position or role in society. The view of the taskforce is that it would be beneficial if people in the second half of their careers could combine work with educational, cultural or voluntary activities, as this reduces physical and mental stress. This will reap benefits both at the end of a person's working life and in the twenty years or so which people still have before them when they finally stop working.

The taskforce placed particular emphasis on:

- investing in career path planning for people in the 45-55 age range;
- introducing job rotation as a right;
- combining work with education, family care and voluntary work;
- supporting re-evaluation and the realisation of ambitions;
- the prevention of work disability;
- career development as opposed to retirement;
- enabling access to information technology and computing training courses;
- combining paid and unpaid work in high 'burn out' professions;
- focusing 'About to Retire' courses on continuity and new challenges;
- creating temporary employment opportunities for employees who are no longer part of the regular workforce;
- offering companies continuity in the form of pools of older specialist personnel;
- developing entrepreneurial skills at a more advanced age.

The battle against well-worn paths

The taskforce is interested in examining the effect of new working methods and approaches, and methods for changing attitudes and involving older people in the workforce again. The public sector areas of education and healthcare have been identified by the taskforce for trials. In these sectors the demand for personnel is most acute, as there is a constant exodus of personnel and the short-term choices of the relevant employers. In addition, the taskforce would like to invite branches of industry or regions to volunteer to become pilots for innovative approaches.

Suggested innovative approaches are:

- regional support to companies on age-related and diversity policies;
- older mentors for new entrepreneurs and young employees;
- encouraging mature people to start new businesses;
- time management and combining work with other activities;
- refresher courses for professionals in the areas of personnel work, employment, working conditions and the media.

The taskforce is aware that it has to combine its aspirations with a practical and realistic approach. Its aim is also to ensure the most effective involvement of all the relevant parties. The evaluation methods that can be used to monitor progress will also be specified. Further activities will be defined as its work progress.

4

Retirement policies

Removing incentives to early retirement and encouraging later retirement

It is perhaps this area of public policy that is most developed in the countries studied. Later retirement is being encouraged in all of the countries, although the view was expressed that this was an area in which policies needed to be developed further. For example, in Australia there are now incentives for an individual to defer drawing their pension until age 70. In Finland, companies are required to make a contribution to the costs of disability pensions, which one informant suggested might make them reluctant to take on older workers. Also in Finland, the unemployment route to retirement, whereby an individual could move on to unemployment benefits at the age of 53 has been modified such that the age of entry is now 55. In Finland, outflow rates from unemployment among older workers are low and it was proposed that once on this pathway it is difficult to motivate individuals to participate in active labour market programmes.

In Japan, the age at which an individual can claim a basic pension is being increased – it rose from age 60 to age 61 in April 2001 and will gradually rise until, in 2013, it will not be payable until the worker reaches age 65. Although the salary-linked portion is still paid at age 60, there are also plans for this to be paid at age 65 in the future (Fujimura, 2001, p 1; Kimura and Oka, 2001, p 353). According to informants, this was problematic because there had not initially been discussions with the Ministry of Labour about the labour market implications. Currently, a substantial majority of Japanese firms operate a mandatory retirement age of 60 (Fujimura, 2001, p 6), although legislation passed in 1994 requires

employers to try to retain workers until the age of 65 (Kimura and Oka, 2001, p 351). Japanese public policy on age and employment is primarily targeted at older men in lifetime employment, from which the majority of women are excluded (Kimura and Oka, 2001, p 350).

In large firms, the most commonly adopted response to government requests to extend working life has been to extend employment beyond mandatory age at 60 but to leave present personnel systems largely intact (Fujimura, 2001, p 7). Recently, many large firms have adopted a system of continued employment after mandatory retirement. One such approach taken by Matsushita Electric Industrial Co Ltd is discussed below (page 23).

Also in Japan, the income test on receipt of a pension while working, which discouraged employment after the age of 60, was substantially raised in 1995 (Koshiro, 1996, p 98; Kimura and Oka, 2001, p 352).

In the Netherlands, firms are increasingly moving away from early retirement (VUT) schemes to pre-pension schemes that are capital funded. The government is emphasising the need to discourage early retirement, to encourage the participation of those aged 55-65, to make work more attractive, to prevent involuntary retirement and to give the responsibility for funding early retirement to individuals (Ministry for Social Affairs and Employment, undated, pp 16-17). One aspect of this policy has been the ending, in 1999, of the exemption of unemployed people aged 57.5 or over from the requirement to work. People over 57.5 are now required to register at an employment office and must accept suitable employment opportunities. However, they are not required to actively seek a job (Ministry for

Social Affairs and Employment, 2001, p 6). One informant felt that, in response to such initiatives, many individuals would simply adjust their retirement planning so that they could still retire early. Those who could afford to would still do so, while those who might prefer to retire would be forced to remain economically active because, for example, they entered employment late or made choices earlier on in their careers that were now detrimental.

In the USA, the age at which a social security pension can be claimed is gradually being raised to 67 (Rix, 2001) with penalties for early retirement, and there is a current debate regarding accelerating this process. Also, limits on what a person can earn before their benefits are affected are being relaxed, and there will be a gradual increase in the retirement credit paid to workers delaying retirement until age 70 (Rix, 2001, p 388). In addition, it is now possible for older workers to continue to work and continue to claim some of their disability benefits. Another idea being considered is allowing an individual to draw on some of their occupational pension and continue to work.

A respondent made similar points to those concerning the Netherlands (see above). In their view, pension reforms in the USA, in particular the trend towards defined contribution over defined benefit plans, will result in much greater diversity in the ages at which people retire. People who have made better choices, are better educated and can contribute more will be in a better situation to retire early than if they were in a defined benefit scheme. On the other hand, others may spend their resources on consumption rather than a pension and may be forced to continue to work, whereas under a defined benefit plan those resources would have been guaranteed.

Ending mandatory retirement

In Australia the abolition of mandatory retirement in all states by 1999 (Encel, 2000a) has apparently had little impact to date. The rate of involuntary retirement continues as before; employers find other ways to retire older workers and the rate of voluntary retirement encouraged by superannuation also continues to be high. Similarly, in the USA in the past few years there

has been a slight decline in early retirement (before age 65), but this was considered to be due to the decline of defined benefit pension schemes rather than to the elimination of mandatory retirement (since most people retired before that even became an issue).

Gradual retirement schemes

A discussion of gradual retirement could have been included in the discussion of pension reform, but its importance in recent debates means that it merits separate discussion. There would appear to be a strong case for the introduction of gradual retirement: for employers it offers the possibility of skill and knowledge retention, while for older workers it offers the opportunity for a gradual adjustment to retirement. Yet gradual retirement has not met with the success its proponents had anticipated. Take up has sometimes been low and, arguably, it is simply another form of early retirement. For example, the Finnish government is against the continuation of its scheme because part-time workers contribute less to the economy, government is required to make a financial contribution and there are labour shortages in some sectors of the economy. The system also favours higher earners. Finally, the reorganisation of jobs required to accommodate part-time pensioners is not always practical in some sectors, and employers are not always satisfied with the arrangements. One respondent referred to recent research which indicated that, had gradual retirement not been available, half of claimants would have continued in full-time work, while the other half would have exited via full early retirement. Thus, the net effect of gradual retirement had not been to raise participation rates.

This is in contrast to Japan, where versions of gradual retirement are now available and take up has been relatively high. The difference between Japan and Europe perhaps reflects the backgrounds to these various initiatives. In European countries there has been a long-term emphasis on early exit, with relatively generous retirement benefits available, while in Japan early retirement has never been the norm.

An important issue that emerges from examining retirement in Japan is that of institutionalised ageism. For example, Matsushita Electric Industrial Co Ltd is a large firm, which has implemented a re-employment scheme in response to the increase of Japan's public pension eligibility age. Under the terms of this scheme a relatively low wage is supplemented by pension income, leaving an individual somewhat better off than if they had opted for retirement at 60. Workers can work until age 65, although their contract is reviewed annually. By March 2001, 307 (36.7%) of those reaching age 60 chose to join the programme, indicating that it was not attractive to most people. Reasons include consideration of income difference between work or non-work and the quality of re-employment work. Of these, only 201 (65.5%) were re-employed, mainly due to a shortage of available jobs. The scheme could simply be viewed as shifting older workers into publicly subsidised low pay work. While it may be a stepping-stone towards later retirement, it may also institutionalise age-discrimination as those over the age of 60 are treated differently from other workers (Taylor et al, 2002). Such arrangements could be viewed as embedding age barriers further rather than removing them and encouraging further age discrimination. A more pragmatic view is that such schemes accept the existence of age barriers in the labour market and at least offer some older workers the opportunity to remain economically active.

In the USA, the number of older workers in some form of bridge employment between a career job and full retirement is large. However, the number of workers moving into such jobs via formal programmes within their companies is rare. Thus, workers usually obtain such employment of their own volition. Mobility is often (although not exclusively) downward (Rix, 2001, p 383).

5

Age discrimination

Legislation, protection against dismissal and age bars in recruitment

Three of the countries studied – Australia, Finland and the USA – already have legislation proscribing anti-age discrimination legislation in employment. The legislative provisions of these countries have already been discussed at length in a recent JRF report (Hornstein et al, 2001) and will therefore not be discussed here.

In Japan, the Employment Measures Law has been amended and, since October 2001, companies have been requested to carry out recruitment and hiring activities without reference to age. Also, employment offices will not take job advertisements that carry age limits. 'Guidelines to abolish age discrimination' (*Japan Labour Bulletin*, 2001b) specify circumstances under which age limits in recruitment are permitted, including:

1. Workers in specific age groups, such as new graduates, for the purpose of career development over long tenure.
2. Workers in specific age groups because it is necessary for companies to maintain or restore the demographic structure of their workforce for the purpose of maintaining business activities or passing on skills and knowledge.
3. Workers under a certain age with consideration to a mandatory retirement age or maximum age, and for the periods necessary for new workers to demonstrate their abilities and to build up professional skills.
4. Workers under a certain age when, in order to make wage payments regardless of age to new employees, companies will be required to revise present regulations determining wages, mainly in accordance with age.

5. Workers in specific age groups because company sales or service activities are aimed at specific age groups.
6. Workers in specific age groups in the art and entertainment fields.
7. Workers under a certain age because the duties necessitate a certain physical condition.
8. Where jobs are deemed to be for existing middle-aged and older workers in line with administrative policies.
9. Duties whose execution is prohibited or restricted to workers in specific age groups.

There have been objections to these guidelines, with some arguing that any exceptions are unjustifiable and opposing age limits linked to seniority systems, although the MHLW has expressed the view that exceptions should be allowed in order to remain in line with existing employment practices. Moreover, the law simply states that "employers should make efforts not to exclude the workers in question from recruiting or hiring due to their age" (*Japan Labour Bulletin*, 2001b), and thus does not impose any penalty for violation. The guidelines conclude by emphasising the need for future revisions to take account of the social and economic situation at the time.

In Japan, it is now possible for a firm to offer a temporary contract of more than one year to workers aged 60 and over. This does not apply to workers under the age of 60 who can either be offered a one-year or permanent contract. However, it is possible that such regulations may discourage firms from recruiting workers aged under 60.

Additionally, in Japan the Law for the Stabilisation of Employment of Older Persons requires companies to provide support to middle-aged and older workers who leave their jobs due to forced retirement or redundancy, in the form of outplacement and training, days off for job-seeking, recruitment information, recommendations to related companies and developing collaborations with other companies. Public Employment Security Offices provide grants to employers to help them undertake these activities (Iwata, 2001).

In the Netherlands the government has introduced financial penalties for firms that dismiss older workers. However, the view of one respondent was that firms were willing to pay to reduce the numbers of older workers they employ and recruit less expensive and more productive (that is, younger) workers, while another felt that this would simply encourage firms to dismiss older workers sooner.

Raising awareness

Education and awareness raising campaigns have been implemented in Australia, Finland, Germany and the Netherlands. These have targeted both older people and employers. For example, the government of Queensland in Australia has produced a booklet and a website – 'A guide to retiring' (Queensland Government Department of Families, 2000; http://www.families.qld.gov.au/retirement/) – which aims to help older people plan for their future and make informed lifestyle decisions.

A national campaign in Germany – 50 Plus, They Know What to Do – has also aimed to raise awareness of age discrimination among employers. This has included a brochure and a media campaign. In addition, local employment offices approach employers directly with the resumes of individual older workers.

The view of an individual representing the Dutch taskforce on ageing workers was that changing attitudes towards older workers among employers was the key to successfully implementing public policies on age and employment. Unless employers were favourably disposed to older workers, policies would not be optimally effective. However, such attitudes are often not articulated or recognised by managers and are therefore difficult to tackle.

6

Employment and training programmes

Employment policy has tended to lag behind social welfare and pension reform in addressing issues associated with population ageing. However, a small employment programme has existed in the USA for a number of years and others are emerging in the other case study countries. In Finland it is possible for an individual to enter adult education while claiming full unemployment benefits. However, take-up has been low and one respondent suggested that this is because people require considerable support in entering education and during their studies.

In New South Wales, Australia, since 1990 the Mature Workers Program has offered services for people aged over 40 and looking for a job. Target groups are people:

- out of the workforce and wanting to return to work;
- looking to update their skills;
- recently made redundant and looking for work;
- wanting to change career;
- retired, but wanting to return to the workforce.

Services offered include advice on skill needs, training, practical assistance in job-search and interview skills, and work experience. The employment element of the programme is provided by community organisations, while the training element is provided by private contractors and public sector organisations. Evidence suggests that the scheme has had some success, with two thirds (approximately 65%) of clients finding work in 1993/94. The majority attributed their success at least in part to the programme (Encel, 2000a, p 11, 2000b, p 237).

Western Australia has launched a similar programme under the banner Profit from Experience. The scheme targets those aged 45 or over who are unemployed, under-employed or soon to be made redundant and not receiving Commonwealth assistance. It is an early intervention scheme with the primary focus on people who have been out of employment for between three and 12 months.

Older workers are supported by a network of access officers who provide employment counselling, support, advice and introductions to employers. Providers are given flexibility in how they deliver the programme in order to meet the needs of their particular client group. Assistance to older jobseekers is provided within a number of separate but complimentary elements of the programme. In the training element additional workplace supervision or training can also be paid for while an individual is starting a job.

The elements of the programme are as follows:

- a network of support officers providing personal assistance and advice;
- assistance to equip individuals to get back to work;
- assistance to identify and explore work options;
- recognition of current skills.

The majority of clients have not been registered unemployed, but rather have retired but wish to return to work. An evaluation of the services delivered by five providers found that benefits of the programme identified by clients were: restoring self-esteem, confidence or support; training in the use of information and communication technologies; direct links to employment or casual work; and help with preparing a curriculum vitae. Placement rates have been highest among the 45-50 age group.

However, age barriers to the employment of clients have been recognised as a problem and, thus, the scope of the programme was broadened in 2001 to include changing attitudes among employers. The approach was for community-based employment agencies – Job Links – to target employers, employer bodies and recruitment agencies in their area rather than undertaking a costly marketing campaign.

In Germany in March 2001, representatives of the German federal government, trades unions and employers' associations met under the umbrella of the national Alliance for Jobs, Training and Competitiveness. Participants agreed on a programme to improve the employment prospects of older workers. In a memorandum participants outlined a partial revision of earlier policies concerning early and partial retirement: while earlier programmes primarily focused on reducing the number of older employees in the workforce, the new initiative seeks to reduce unemployment among older workers. The following measures were agreed:

- The Federal Employment Service (Bundesanstalt für Arbeit) will provide co-funding for job-related training in small- and medium-sized companies with not more than 100 employees. Funding will be provided for up to four years.
- The age limit for employees to be eligible for certain types of wage subsidies (Eingliederungszuschüsse) will be reduced from 55 years to 50.
- Companies and workers will be educated about the need for life-long learning.
- New training courses will be developed at company level, which fit the needs of older employees.

The Alliance also agreed on guidelines to raise the qualification level of the entire workforce, including older workers (Eironline, 2001). However, informants commented that, at the same time, Germany's partial retirement law is being used to retire older workers early.

In Germany, local employment offices are required to support older workers via offers of training, job placements and subsidies to employers. However, the focus is on those aged between 50 and 55, as it is considered that their prospects of re-employment are better. Nonetheless, this represents a change in government policy. Previously, training could only be provided if it was considered that there was a chance it would be successful in improving an individual's employment prospects. This meant that training was seldom offered to older workers. Recently, employment offices have begun to view older workers in a differentiated way, considering which older workers are trainable or employable, rather than assuming older workers are an homogenous group.

In Japan, Career Exchange Plazas aim to help unemployed white-collar workers aged 45 years and over re-enter employment. These are administered by the Associations of Employment Development for Senior Citizens, which operate in each prefecture. They provide consultancy advice for firms regarding the employment of older workers, and assist older workers in updating their skills and career management. Career Exchange Plazas were launched in 1999 and provide up to 12 weeks of support and assistance in job-seeking, including personal counselling, training in interview skills, use of a computer, preparing a curriculum vitae and voluntary meetings among members so that they can share experiences. Clients must be registered with Human Resource Banks – sections of the Public Employment Security Offices that specialise in job-placement services aimed exclusively at older workers. Clients are given the use of computers, fax machines and telephones. Currently, over 5,000 older jobseekers per year are assisted in 12 areas (Naganawa, 2002).

The Tokyo Career Exchange Plaza achieves a 40% job placement rate, which is higher than the average for the age group. However, in considering the purpose and effectiveness of such initiatives it is important to consider the issue of deadweight. It has been pointed out that, in Tokyo, professional and technical workers are in high demand, which suggests that such rates might not be repeated elsewhere. Another issue to consider is that of additionality, as clients are also required to be registered with Human Resource Banks and are in fact sometimes co-located with Career Exchange Plazas, these no doubt also contribute to their placement prospects (Naganawa, 2002). Thus, it is difficult to disentangle the area-specific effects, although training in preparation for re-employment, including the use of personal computers and opportunities for members to share and exchange their experiences, which are unique to Career Exchange Plazas, appear to be particularly useful for older workers (Naganawa, 2002). Nonetheless, it is difficult to see much in this particular initiative that would not usually be offered by programmes targeting guidance, support and training at unemployed people in general. It is unclear therefore why a specific programme targeting older, white-collar jobseekers is provided. Also in Japan, public employment offices have organised job fairs specifically for older workers.

Above it was noted that Japanese public policy aims to supply diverse work opportunities for those over the age of 60. In this regard, Silver Human Resource Centres (SHRCs) offer temporary and short-term work opportunities for retirees aged 60 and over. They are designed to provide a combination of work, a modest income, personal enrichment and social purpose for older people as well as contributing to the community. There are 1,328 centres nationwide with a total membership of 540,000 as of 1998.

Also in Japan, government subsidies are available to companies that provide training for people aged 45 or over, while the government also aims to extend guidance services to adults. Japan recently launched a scheme providing support to groups of three people aged over 60 who join together to launch a small business.

In the Netherlands, tax incentives are available to firms that train older workers.

In the USA, while reforms are underway that aim to extend working life and legislation against age discrimination has been in place for some considerable time, labour market policy towards older workers is not well developed. Respondents expressed the view that this issue was not high on the policy agenda. A job placement programme – Senior Community Service Employment Program (SCSEP) – assisting severely disadvantaged older workers aged 55 or over helps only a very small proportion of those eligible, and there are no plans to increase its coverage. In fact, its budget has declined in real terms in recent years. SCSEP aims to help low-income individuals with poor employment prospects into part-time positions in community-based work. The Department of Labor regulations specify a target of placing 20% of clients in unsubsidised positions (Support Services International, undated, p 2).

The 1998 Workforce Investment Act (WIA) aims to consolidate and streamline federal employment programmes, and provide states and localities with greater discretion in terms of developing labour force development strategies that meet their local needs. A feature of the WIA is universal access, although low-income individuals and welfare recipients are prioritised. The WIA requires states to provide one-stop delivery systems that integrate services provided under the WIA and by SCSEP. Under the WIA, local systems may include 'one-stop partners', which serve particular populations and can receive funds via the WIA. Such partners may include organisations serving the needs of older workers, although the WIA emphasises that service providers are selected on a competitive basis by Workforce Investment Boards (WIBs), which are given the task of developing and operating systems that best meet the needs of their areas. SCSEP may remain separate from the one-stop centre, although a mechanism must exist whereby clients utilising the centre can access SCSEP.

However, several respondents felt that the WIA may actually have undermined the provision of training for unemployed older workers. For example, membership of WIBs does not require the involvement of the State Unit on Aging or SCSEP grantees, although consideration of their involvement is expected and the involvement of lead state agencies is required. Additionally, specific funds targeting older workers have been ended, although states may reserve funds for state-wide activities that specifically target older workers (Kramer and Smith Nightingale, 2001, pp 10-11). It was also felt that one-stop centres were too youth oriented.

On the other hand, older workers were substantially under-represented in the provision that the WIA replaced (Poulos and Smith Nightingale, 1997, p iii; Kramer and Smith Nightingale, 2001, p 12). One respondent pointed out that funds were under-spent in the past, perhaps because the training on offer did not meet the needs of many of the client group. Under the terms of the WIA, states are required to develop Workforce Investment Plans that should consider the coordination and non-duplication of services (Kramer and Smith Nightingale, 2001, p 11). The WIA also establishes a performance accountability system that requires states and WIBs to report on special populations, including older workers. In addition to employment outcomes, states are also required to report on indicators of client satisfaction (Kramer and Smith Nightingale, 2001, p 15).

While the view was that the issue of age and employment was not high on the federal government's agenda, reports and guidance materials on employment and the provision of training and job placements for older workers have been issued by the Department of Labor in recent years. Three manuals have been produced by the Employment and Training Administration of the US Department of Labor, which aim to increase unsubsidised job placement rates.

First, *Placing SCSEP enrollees in unsubsidized employment: A summary of best practice in successful programs* (Support Services International, undated) identifies the following characteristics of more successful programmes:

- clients and potential host agencies are made aware that job-placement is a central goal;
- projects prioritise the development of relationships with local employers and are creative in finding job placements;
- projects place responsibility for finding and keeping a job with the client; collaboration among clients is encouraged;
- projects look for job openings all year round; clients may be taken on prospective visits to employers;
- projects network more with other local resources;
- projects employ a variety of approaches to challenge clients' expectations and increase self-confidence;
- projects are also better at assessing the aptitudes and interests of clients and matching these to jobs;
- projects make considerable use of the media in stimulating interest in SCSEP;
- projects undertake effective post-placement follow-up.

Second, *Using motivation and training to increase job placements* (National Senior Citizens Education and Research Center, 1998) outlines how SCSEP providers can create a motivational environment for clients, use the process of assessment to increase motivation, use motivational techniques, the role of skills training, and the relationship between SCSEP and vocational education programmes.

Third, *Using public relations to market older workers* (National Senior Citizens Education and Research Centre, undated).

While the practical advice provided in these three documents is no doubt of use to providers of services to older workers, it could be argued that much of the content would also be helpful to providers of similar services to other disadvantaged groups. The reports are generally not specific to the needs of older workers, other than the second publication's discussion of the relationship between SCSEP and other older worker specific programmes and the third report's discussion of the appropriate language to use in promotional materials for job fairs for older workers.

However, further reports issued by the Division of Older Worker Programs, Employment and Training Administration, US Department of Labor (Polous and Smith Nightingale, 1997; Kramer, 2001) do alert training providers to demographic trends and their implications for the design and delivery of services. These reports consider the policy implications of increasing numbers of older people, the implications of the ageing population for service delivery and the needs of particular sub-groups.

Also in the USA, The National Older Worker Career Center (NOWCC) – a not-for-profit organisation established in Washington, DC in 1997 – aims to:

1. expand employment and training opportunities for workers aged over 40, through forming partnerships with public and private organisations to expand employment and training opportunities;
2. encourage workplace options that will attract and keep older people in the workforce;
3. promote the message that private and public policies and programmes must reflect demographic and job market realities;
4. advocate for an age-diverse workforce and employer policies, practices and programmes based on the principle of equal treatment of workers of all ages.

NOWCC argues that these programmes and policies should balance retention and recruitment of older workers with training and development opportunities for workers of all ages.

NOWCC offers private and public employers skilled and experienced workers age 40 and over through ExperTemp, a temporary employment agency that works on assignments of more than 45 days and supplies candidates seeking regular positions. Employee duties and professional qualifications, geographic location and other factors affect the fees that are charged. No fee is charged if temporary employees move into permanent positions and have worked for a reasonable period of time subject to negotiation.

The National Senior Citizens Education and Research Center Inc (NSCERC) was incorporated in 1962, in the District of Columbia, as a not-for-profit organisation. NSCERC provides employment for older people via SCSEP and Career Opportunities for Experienced Workers (COEW). The latter is a contextual learning project and operates in the Fort Worth area of Texas. The project is outlined in Box 3.

NOWCC and NSCERC both operate the Senior Environmental Employment (SEE) programme. Established in 1976, funded by the US Environmental Protection Agency and operated nationwide, this programme provides full-time and part-time opportunities for individuals age 55 and over. The programme offers short-term, renewable assignments that include office reception, editing, technical writing, engineering and science. Clients assist in a wide variety of projects at federal, state and local environmental offices and laboratories. Depending on work assignment details, participants receive fully paid health insurance, holiday, sick leave and other benefits.

Also in the USA are groups representing older people from minority ethnic groups, and some of their activities include support with finding employment. For instance, the National Association for Hispanic Elderly and the National Indian Council on Aging administer SCSEP programmes, while the National Asian Pacific Center on Aging and the National Caucus and Center on Black Aged Inc administer both SCSEP and SEE programmes.

While specific initiatives targeting older workers are emerging, a view among some informants was that public employment offices were required to undertake too many initiatives and campaigns relating to youth, unemployed women, disabled people and older workers, as well as managing reorganisations and introducing quality management measures. Given that supporting older workers can be time consuming, it was felt that older workers might not receive the support they need.

Box 3: Career Opportunities for Experienced Workers (COEW) (USA)

Career Opportunities for Experienced Workers (COEW) is targeted at dislocated workers who are aged 40 or older and have at least one of the following characteristics:

- limited proficiency in English;
- low basic skills;
- multiple barriers to employment, including health, personal and educational credentials;
- obsolete or minimal transferable skills;
- interim employed, based on low wage recovery rate and inconsistencies with career goals.

The programme is operated in four phases:

1. Workforce literacy training (three weeks – 120 hours in the classroom).
2. Self-paced occupational or workplace skills training (80 hours) combined with on-the-job training/job shadowing/career development training and continued basic skills (80 hours). This phase takes four weeks.
3. Placement/on-the-job training, post-employment support, continued basic skills.
4. Post-employment support and continuing education.

Although there are numerous partners, the programme is operated primarily by Tarrant County Junior College, which provides the instructors for the courses, and the National Senior Citizens Education and Research Center, which is responsible for programme development, recruitment, assessment, counselling, job development and placement. The programme began enrolling participants in June 2000.

The counsellors, who are located in the building, provide a highly supportive environment for finding a job. The curriculum meets the demands of the labour market by requiring most of the lessons to be carried out on a computer.

COEW collaborates with a number of partner organisations, including the Tarrant County Central Labor Council, Tarrant County College District, Work Advantage (the local WIB), Fort Worth Opportunity Center, Fort Worth Hispanic Chamber of Commerce and the Vietnamese Women's Association. The instructors that provide the basic and occupational skills training have been teaching for many years at various levels and have extensive experience in teaching participants in this age group.

The facility in which the counsellors and participant training activity is housed is particularly good. Located central to a low-income, immigrant community, the Fort Worth Opportunity Center is a spacious, high-tech building that is aesthetically pleasing and creates a very comfortable learning environment. Each classroom is equipped with a computer terminal for each student.

Students appear to have open and personal relationships with the counsellors. Likewise, the counsellors have a high level of familiarity with each of the students, their backgrounds and their expectations for themselves and the programme. This relationship creates a supportive environment in which the participants can feel comfortable to succeed.

Targeting of low-skilled, limited English-speaking population

Approximately 30% of participants are limited English-speaking and most have low basic skills. The recruitment materials that COEW has developed are written in English and Spanish, with plans to translate them into Vietnamese. Recruitment methods that COEW is using include:

- advertisements on Vietnamese radio and on television;
- promotional materials at the Hispanic Chamber of Commerce;
- word of mouth, particularly with the Central Labor Council.

All recruitment materials are positive, informative and encouraging. Participants hear about COEW by word of mouth, through Work Advantage and through local newspapers.

The location of the project coordinator's office in the offices of the Central Labor Council also provides the opportunity for COEW to reach eligible participants through referral. Employers who are members of the Central Labor Council, some of whom may be experiencing layoffs or plant closings, are aware of the opportunity for their employees to receive COEW's services for re-employment.

The programme is designed for 10 cycles of 15 participants and that number of participants was easily achieved in the first three cycles.

Use of contextual learning strategies

Programme design

The first three weeks of the programme are dedicated to refreshing participants' basic skills and introducing them to the computer and its basic applications. The curriculum for the basic skills training is well developed and thorough. While three weeks is a very short time in which to get through the material, the instructors appear to be very pleased with the students' ability to understand it. Minor revisions have been made to the curriculum for the following cycles, most of which are in the nature of spending more time on some topics (such as the use of Windows) and less time on others (such as stress management).

After the first three weeks, students receive more computer or occupational skills training and either on-the-job training or job shadowing with an employer or more work in the classroom on job-search skills. During this time, participants have individual meetings with their counsellor to identify the types of jobs in which they are interested. Participants appear to have very clear ideas and preferences about the work they are interested in pursuing and, according to the programme staff, these expectations are pragmatic.

Contextual learning strategies

As mentioned above, each participant is exposed to brief but intense basic skills and occupational skills training. The age of participants (40 and over) has a significant impact on their attitudes about the importance of training. It also allows for the development of camaraderie and mutual respect for one another. Since the lessons are primarily carried out on the computer, participants get further experience and familiarity in using computers, while at the same time reviewing and refining basic skills.

The instructors teaching the courses have extensive experience in teaching adults and relating the material to concepts relevant to older people. This programme provides an introduction to the new occupational skills that are valued in the labour market, then encourages participants to pursue jobs where they can put those new skills to work – after only three weeks. It is designed to get people back to work almost immediately and aims for participants to spend the minimum amount of time out of a job. In addition, the programme focuses on the manufacturing and service industries and the curriculum is therefore designed to teach skills that are most valuable to employers in those industries.

Placement and post-placement strategies

The Program Coordinator and counsellors are heavily involved in contacting employers and setting up interviews for participants. With the location of the programme near the Fort Worth Opportunity Center, the programme operators have the opportunity to develop ongoing beneficial relationships with local employers. The proximity allows employers to see first-hand the level of skill and instruction that participants are getting and, at the same time, participants have access to on-the-job training and job shadowing opportunities with the FWOC employers. One problem that the programme operator is preparing to face is employer impatience with the length of the programme. The fear is that employers will want to hire participants full-time before they complete the programme.

Customer satisfaction methods

COEW has prepared a customer satisfaction questionnaire for participants to fill out on completion of the programme. The programme has an ongoing quality improvement process and suggestions are taken seriously. The counsellors also meet with participants once each week to discuss their situation.

Support to employers

Advice, guidance, training and employment placements

Specific support to business, to smaller firms in particular, in implementing age-friendly human resource management policies is not much in evidence in the countries studied. The Finnish Programme on Ageing Workers included the provision of free support in developing age-friendly policies to small- and medium-sized firms with at least 40% of their workforce aged over 45. Forthcoming Australian proposals may also include such activities, but expanded to also cover other diversity issues.

In Germany a small project has involved the transfer of good practice in age management into companies. The project worked with five companies over an 18-month period, helping them to implement policies. The companies were not interested in applying external models but preferred assistance that would help them in tackling the specific problems they faced.

Also, a new federal initiative in Germany is aimed at the recruitment of 3,000 new outreach project workers to employment offices whose role will be to increase the employability of older unemployed people and promote them to businesses. The aim is to directly bring unemployed older workers closer to employing companies. One respondent referred to German research that had found a successful approach to be the use of active mechanisms whereby older workers are put in contact with companies, for example, via work placements and probation periods.

In the Netherlands, its association of personnel managers has a code of practice on recruitment that refers to age discrimination.

In Finland, the Netherlands and the USA age awareness training courses and seminars have been provided for trainers, personnel officers and managers in firms.

The Employment and Training Administration of the US Department of Labor has produced a *Supervisor's guide* on managing ageing workers (McIntosh, 2001a). This guide, while ostensibly focusing on what supervisors need to know, discusses areas such as job rotation, sabbaticals, benefits, hours of employment, teleworking, retirement, establishing a 'learning environment' and the creation of mentoring or liaison positions across departments, all of which they are likely to have almost no influence over. Also implicit in the document is an assumption that its audience is supervisors in larger firms. The guide also says almost nothing about *how* such changes can be achieved.

In addition, *An employer's guide to older workers* (McIntosh, 2001b) has been produced. Again, the document is deficient in a number of areas, the first of which is presentation. It is somewhat 'academic', including references to the authors of various academic texts throughout. A further deficiency is that, although published in 2001, it is already somewhat dated – its starting point is that firms are facing labour shortages, when for many US firms this is no longer the case. The document also has a tendency to contrast the so-called qualities of older workers with the deficiencies of younger ones, for example, the former are identified in quoted research as being more committed and cost the same or less to train (McIntosh, 2001b, p 5). Messages in the document are also unclear. For example, it refers to "this under-appreciated and under-utilized segment of the labour force" (McIntosh, 2001, p 7), while previously reporting that employers associate a number of positive qualities with older workers. The final, but perhaps most important deficiency is the emphasis in the document on 'older workers', rather than focusing on policies to promote effective 'age management' in firms, despite emphasising the limited value of chronological age in determining which human resource management policies should be applied (McIntosh, 2001, p 13).

However, the document does provide some potentially valuable information, for example strategies for targeting recruitment drives at older people, for communicating effectively, for making work more flexible and for making training more accessible, although the document is also partial in its coverage of these issues. For example, age discrimination in selection and career management are important issues that are not discussed. Again, there appears to be an emphasis on larger firms.

Support to labour market intermediaries

As has already been noted, specific support for labour market intermediaries in working with employers and older workers has been an integral part of the Finnish Programme on Ageing Workers. Also, in Germany, a brochure on the employment of older workers has been distributed to people involved in providing labour market advice, and a current major research programme includes projects working with intermediaries. Australian proposals may also include such activities and a small intervention fund is available on which intermediaries can draw to help support innovative activities at the local level. The Netherlands' employment agency has an anti-discrimination code in which age is incorporated, although one respondent felt that awareness of this among officials was low.

In the USA the National Association of Older Worker Employment Services (NAOWES) was created in 1981, and is devoted to supporting older worker employment services professionals. NAOWES aims to:

- improve employment opportunities for older workers;
- promote understanding of their capabilities and dispel myths;

- serve as an advocate for older workers and older worker employment services;
- involve private industry in Association business;
- identify the training needs of older workers;
- provide technical assistance, information exchange, training and a forum for discussion of older worker issues.

Employment incentive schemes

Wage subsidies have been popular in some of the countries studied and these exist for both older workers and employers, although respondents questioned the value of this approach. For example, a system of subsidised placements exists in Finland and the view of one respondent was that placements were hard to find for most clients, except those who were highly qualified and who might expect to find employment anyway.

Also, in Germany, firms recruiting a worker aged 50 or over who has been unemployed for 12 months or more can receive a subsidy equivalent to 50% of the person's wages for up to two years and in certain circumstances longer. In Bavaria, one scheme provides a subsidy to firms that recruit a worker aged 50 or over to a temporarily vacant position for 12 months. Such schemes are generally not applied after the age of 55 and affect only small numbers of older workers, partly because at the age of 58 unemployed workers can claim an early pension and are not obliged to look for work.

Against a background of record levels of unemployment, wage subsidies in Japan are available to firms that recruit unemployed middle-aged and older workers. The Special Grant for Emergency Employment Creation subsidises firms that recruit workers aged 45-59. Another scheme – Grants for Employment Development for Specified Job Applicants – is aimed at firms recruiting disabled workers aged 55 or over. A revised version of this scheme was to be implemented in October 2001 limiting coverage to those aged 60 or over. However, instead, an emergency measure was included in the programme, which stipulated that if unemployment rose above 5% the age of eligibility would be lowered to 45 (*Japan Labour Bulletin*, 2001c), potentially disadvantaging those who are older, as firms might be more inclined to recruit those at the lower end of the eligibility age range.

Also, under a previous version of the Special Incentive Money for Employment Creation in New and Growing Fields programme, only 30- to 59-year-olds were eligible, and firms recruiting 45- to 59-year-olds received ¥700,000, compared to ¥400,000 if the firm recruited a 30- to 44-year-old. However, under a new version of the scheme the amount received by the firm (¥700,000) is the same whatever the age of the recruit (Human Resource Development Bureau, 2000, p 5). It could be argued that this change might make firms less likely to recruit older workers, as there is no longer a particular incentive to do so.

Also in Japan, the Benefit for the Aged whose Continue to Work provides a wage top-up to people aged 60-64 who continue to work or resume work a short period after teinen (retirement), and who are receiving up to 85% of the average wage they were receiving six months prior to teinen. The total of the benefit is 25% of the workers' wage. As the workers' wage increases above 80% of their previous wage the percentage is reduced, reaching zero at 85%. An important feature of this scheme is that the subsidy is paid to the worker directly (Kimura and Oka, 2001, p 351).

An employment official in a Japanese public employment office commented that often firms did not retain older workers after a wage subsidy ended and the representative of a Japanese employers' association commented that wage subsidies that were paid to workers directly were more effective.

The government of Queensland in Australia offers the Experience Pays Wage Subsidy of up to Aus$4,400 to employers of eligible jobseekers. Employers who employ a jobseeker aged 45 and over, who has been unemployed for more than 12 months and is not receiving intensive assistance through a Job Network provider or a Disability Employment Service, and who will not displace an existing worker are eligible to apply.

Similarly, South Australia operates two wage subsidy programmes. The Community Employment Assistance Program provides assistance to unemployed people who experience barriers to employment and their target groups include older workers. The programme provides opportunities for vulnerable jobseekers to acquire skills, experience and support in finding employment, and encourages businesses to employ jobseekers via a one-off wage subsidy of Aus$2,000. The Private Sector Employment Program is detailed in Box 4.

In the Netherlands, since 1998 the Jobseekers Employment Act provides a subsidy to employers that recruit long-term unemployed people or provide a work experience placement. The Act does not specifically target older workers. Additionally, from 2002 those that work after the age of 58 can claim tax reductions.

Box 4: Private Sector Employment Program (Australia)

Are you considering taking on a new employee? Could you benefit from receiving financial assistance for a potential new team member? Would you like to contribute to employment growth in South Australia and provide job opportunities for disadvantaged unemployed people? If you answered 'yes' to these questions, you may be eligible for a financial incentive of up to $5,000, through the Private Sector Employment Program. You may also be eligible to receive a training bonus to assist with getting your new employee up to speed.

So what's the Private Sector Employment Program all about?

The Private Sector Employment Program has been developed by the Office of Employment and Youth, and has a commitment from the South Australian government of $12million over the next four years. It is a new programme aimed at supporting employment growth within the South Australian economy by assisting disadvantaged jobseekers.

The program has a two-pronged approach. It targets employers in specific industries to assist them in growing their businesses, as well as jobseekers facing particular barriers to entering the workforce. The greater the disadvantage the jobseeker faces, the higher the incentive the employer will receive in hiring the jobseeker.

Essentially, the programme provides incentives to employers within strategic employment growth areas to create sustainable jobs for disadvantaged jobseekers. Incentives are targeted towards employment growth sectors and industries experiencing current skill shortages, which have the potential to provide sustainable employment.

What's on offer?

The programme works by offering a financial incentive to South Australian employers (in selected industry sectors), of up to $5,000 per employee hired. To access this funding, employers must hire an unemployed worker or a worker recently made redundant for an average of 20 hours or more per week, for a minimum of 12 months. The jobseeker must have been unemployed for at least three months or made redundant within the last three months.

Why does the South Australian government want to help industry and the unemployed?

The government of South Australia has highlighted the importance of continuing to develop the state as a prosperous and vibrant economy. It is a sad fact that unemployment disproportionately affects those groups who may be already socially and economically disadvantaged. The South Australian government, therefore, sees that it is crucial to ensure that disadvantaged groups can participate effectively in labour and training markets in order to both assist people into employment and to achieve the state's social and economic objectives. The Private Sector Employment Program aims to achieve this by targeting the groups considered to be the most disadvantaged in the labour market, with a primary focus on the long-term unemployed.

What industry sectors are targeted?

The Private Sector Employment Program is targeted towards those industry sectors that are contributing to sustained employment growth in South Australia. In considering which industry sectors the Private Sector Employment Program should target, three factors were considered:

- forecast industry growth (that is, greater than the state average)
- skills shortages
- job prospects.

The industry sectors are:

1. Retail/tourism/hospitality (personal and household goods retailing, food and beverage retailing, accommodation, cafés and restaurants)
2. Arts/cultural/recreational/personal services (sports and recreation services, personal services)
3. Property/business services (information technology and computer services, secretarial services, design and multimedia)
4. Manufacturing (food and beverage manufacturing)
5. Community services, health and education (childcare services, age care services, vocational education, medical services).

How can you be eligible for the financial incentive?

Your business must:

- be operating within a targeted industry sector;
- employ an approved voucher holder;
- employ the jobseeker for a minimum of six months to receive a benefit;
- hire the eligible jobseeker for an average of 20 hours or more per week, for a minimum of 12 months in order to receive the full entitlement.

The jobseeker you want to hire must be from a disadvantaged group. Incentive entitlements for disadvantaged unemployed people will be calculated according to the individual's inclusion in various categories, such as:

- length of unemployment;
- whether the individual is of indigenous background;
- whether the person has a disability (intellectual or physical);
- what level of education the jobseeker has;
- age of the jobseeker;
- have been either unemployed for at least three months or made redundant within the last three months.

8

Discussion and implications for public policy

A clear conclusion of this study is that policy making on age and employment is in its infancy, and models and frameworks for the development of policies are only just emerging. As most of the policies discussed in this report are new and the economic background constantly changing, it is difficult to offer an assessment of their impact. Yet what is known about these various initiatives allows some tentative conclusions to be drawn concerning how public policies on age and employment should be designed to maximise their effectiveness. Proposals for the key attributes of such policies are discussed in the sections that follow.

Adequate resources for active measures

It has been noted that governments are moving towards active policies targeting older workers. However, assisting older workers is not a low-cost option. Some older people face multiple barriers that will require an intensive and therefore costly intervention. While encouraging the reintegration and retention of older workers will result in cost savings in terms of pension and social security benefits and increased tax revenues, this will be offset to some extent by the costs associated with training and placing them in employment. Certainly, many employers will be reluctant to pay for the retraining of workers as they age or the redesign of workplaces to make them more age friendly when they can utilise younger workers or even import cheaper labour from or outsource functions to other countries. Some countries are beginning to tackle these issues, although until now there has perhaps been a greater emphasis on pension and social security reform.

Also, over time, a substantial shift away from 'youth'-oriented policy making will be required, particularly with regard to education, to a greater emphasis on life-long learning, age and employment. This is beginning to take place in the countries studied.

Integrated/strategic

The need for the integration of public policies on age and employment has been emphasised throughout this report. Better integration is required both horizontally – that is, across different parts of government – and vertically – that is between government, trades unions, employer bodies, service providers and interest groups. Better horizontal linkages are also required between different aspects of policy on equality, diversity, social exclusion, the family and education, and there is a need to consider the interaction of these factors across the life course. Governments have made limited progress to date, with a fragmentation of policy making and a simplistic approach.

Where perhaps even the most integrated initiatives have been deficient is in terms of often taking 'age' as their starting point, as if this is always an older individual's most important characteristic. This is the case, for example, in Finland's Programme on Ageing Workers. Arguably, ageing issues should be mainstreamed and become part of the activities of all of governments, and considered alongside and in combination with other diversity issues.

Also, pension reform appears to have been the driver of much of the policy making in this area in some of the countries studied, and it could be argued that this has sometimes been undertaken without sufficient consideration of the potential implications for employment policy in particular. For example, whether or not increasing the supply of older workers will be matched by an increase in the demand for them from employers is unclear. There is a potential danger that some older workers will substitute the relative security of early retirement for the insecurity of low pay, contract work or even unemployment. A related point concerns the need to match increasing labour market flexibility with pension reforms. This not only refers to pension portability but also issues such as downshifting late in a career.

Some of these themes are developed further in the following sections.

Non–age-specific

Policy makers in the case study countries have frequently aimed to develop programmes for 'older workers'. Such an approach is simplistic. Chronological age is of limited value in determining the employment-related needs of an individual, and public programmes that use it as a selection criterion may not send the appropriate message to employers and workers. For policy makers used to developing programmes for so-called 'disadvantaged' groups, such as women and minority ethnic groups, the notion of developing and marketing policies for 'older workers' is perhaps appealing, but definitions such as 'older workers' are almost entirely arbitrary. A minority view among the respondents was that, nonetheless, a focus on 'older workers' is merited because of the particular disadvantages they face in the labour market.

The view that interventions should not be age-specific runs counter to that expressed by some age organisations. For example, Australia's Council on the Ageing argues that "services need to be developed specifically for mature workers" (Council on the Ageing, 2001, p 22), including:

- referral to appropriate services and training;
- careers advice;
- assistance with job-search;
- training in using information technology;
- education about the labour market of the 21st century (Council on the Ageing, 2001, p 22).

However, with the exception of transition to retirement programmes, its suggestions for the content of such services do not appear to apply specifically to older workers.

In terms of employment policy, as noted earlier, a greater emphasis on the life course, with attention being given to the factors contributing to labour market disadvantage in later life as proposed by the OECD may be desirable. As age discrimination is not only experienced by people aged over 50 and if a major component of the disadvantages facing older workers are the same as they have faced throughout their adult lives, it is difficult to argue for age group-specific labour market programmes. Remedial actions earlier in a working life may be more effective than interventions that target 'older workers'. Also, policy makers could examine the factors that discourage participation in particular programmes. It may be that the design or delivery mechanism of programmes makes it likely that particular groups would be less likely to participate.

In addition, while there is a risk that by applying, for example, age legislation to all ages (that is, not having an age limit as in the USA's legislation), it could be diluted – it seems paradoxical that legislation outlawing age discrimination can only apply from a certain age.

Perhaps therefore, the particular problems confronting older workers should be acknowledged in terms of service provision, but attention should be paid to the delivery of such services in order to avoid problems such as stigmatisation. Targets might be set for the recruitment of older workers onto particular initiatives, but this does not require the establishing of specific schemes for this group. Initiatives aimed at encouraging the employment of older workers, through, for example, employment incentives, run the risk of deepening age prejudices further and of institutionalising age discrimination. While organisations representing older people have argued for the introduction of schemes aimed to encourage employers to hire older workers on temporary or part-time contracts (Council on the Ageing, 2001, p 17), these may simply disadvantage those seeking permanent full-time positions and encourage firms to consider reducing the wages of older workers in the expectation of obtaining a subsidy. A more positive approach would be to support older workers so that they can obtain the market rate for their labour, for example, by improving workplace design and increasing skill levels among older workers.

At the same time, age-aware employment may also require policy makers to consider the removal of specific employment protection for older workers and to reduce the cost of employing them via encouraging the removal of seniority systems. This point has been made with regard to the USA's Age Discrimination in Employment Act (ADEA), which is argued to have forced some employers to pay older workers more than they are worth. Elsewhere, in Japan for example, mandatory retirement is legal, allowing firms to remove unproductive workers and retain the ones they want, but often on lower wages (Rix, 2001, p 386). That is not to say, however, that all employment protection should be removed, simply that workers could receive a similar level of protection regardless of age.

Another issue concerning the implementation of age-aware employment concerns what constitutes fair and objective performance evaluation if this is the alternative to seniority systems. There is much evidence of age discrimination in workplace performance evaluations (Taylor, 2002). It must also be asked how realistic it would be to expect employers to be willing to implement the sophisticated performance evaluation systems that would be required.

Localised/bottom-up

It was noted in Chapter Three that Finland's Programme on Ageing Workers has been criticised for being too government led. While clearly national government must set the tone for policy towards older workers in terms of incentive structures and employment policy, regional and local government and organisations working on age issues all have a crucial role to play. Initiatives that are specific and local, and undertaken in collaboration with and working through groups representing sectors, occupations, the trades unions, groups campaigning on age issues and community-based organisations, may be perceived as having greater relevance. Moreover, more can be achieved in terms of 'reach' by working through such bodies. Industry, trades union and community-led initiatives will often be perceived

to have greater credibility and thus will have greater impact than those in which government is seen to take the lead. The main roles of government here may be as sponsor, facilitator, coordinator and provider of information, rather than implementer. Also, employer and trades unions groups could be encouraged to develop comprehensive policies on age and employment separate from their involvement in government committees working on this issue.

Unemployed and disabled older workers are often among the most difficult groups to reach. This suggests that programmes should primarily be offered on an outreach basis or near to the target group, as has been attempted in the US Career Opportunities for Experienced Workers initiative referred to earlier (see Box 3, page 31).

For firms this means that ready-made solutions brought from outside will generally be of less value than solutions that, with support, are identified from within and 'owned' by the firm[3]. This will necessitate programmes working with individual firms or sector bodies.

Targeted

There may also be value in considering the issue of age diversity within a wider policy framework for labour force diversity generally. The issue of age itself has been considered above, and it was argued that policy makers must be wary of policies that target heterogeneous groups such as 'older workers'. Rather, policies should be nuanced. Consideration must be given to factors such as gender, disability, socioeconomic group, occupation, sector of employment and length of unemployment. The current fragmentation of policy responses, which, paradoxically, has often resulted in a range of very similar initiatives targeting different so-called disadvantaged groups, has been inefficient and may have weakened their effectiveness.

---

[3] There is evidence for this from outside the case study countries. In Denmark a Senior Fund has been established to support projects in organisations in the private and public sector. An evaluation found that, importantly, it was easier to establish older worker policies that were effective when the project had a firm basis within the company, rather than being initiated from outside.

In raising awareness, consideration should also be given to the widely differing needs of different industries and the problem of influencing the behaviour of firms. General and national programmes of education and awareness-raising may be of limited utility for firms[4].

Flexible

One of the most important features of policy making on age and the labour market must be that it provides people with a degree of choice. It is has been recognised, for example, that pension reforms aimed at extending working life may disadvantage the less well off, forcing them to remain economically active while the better off will be able to continue to retire early (Rix, 2001. pp 388-9). It should be recognised by policy makers that the reintegration of some groups will be problematic at best. Removing early retirement options may mean that some people who perhaps want to and should exit the labour market before pension age may be forced into inappropriate and/or low-paid work or unemployment. In order to be successful, public policies should be capable of meeting the needs of different groups. Thus, it is important that an adequate safety net is available to those for whom employment is an unrealistic option (Council on the Ageing, 2001, p 18).

In the case study countries it is apparent that retirement is becoming much more flexible, which perhaps calls into question the validity of fixed retirement ages. On the other hand, the abolition of mandatory retirement appears to have had little impact. Firms frequently want older workers to retire and many are happy to do so. This may put business and labour at odds with government policy.

In the past it has been relatively easy for firms to target older workers for dismissals, indeed, generous government support has often been available. This has perhaps discouraged the development of policies on age and employment at the company level. Thus, encouraging later exit is not simply a matter of pushing the costs of early retirement onto workers and business. Firms will require substantial support in developing policies on age, while older workers require advice, support and encouragement.

A further and related lesson that can be drawn concerns the kinds of jobs older workers can expect to obtain. It was apparent from the research in Japan, for example, that older workers were sometimes viewed by firms as non-core workers, and care needs to be taken that policies do not only encourage these employment arrangements. While some older workers might be satisfied with such jobs, public policies that encourage the unequal treatment of workers based on their age cannot be viewed as a step towards overcoming age barriers.

Preventive

In the introduction to this report it was noted that the OECD emphasises the need for a preventive approach. As has already been noted, there has been a tendency for public policy to focus on 'older workers'. This is almost certainly too late in some cases, although it is acknowledged that the SCSEP programme in the USA, for instance, has an important role in assisting severely disadvantaged individuals.

In the workplace, preventive support might include grants for implementing job redesign in order to reduce the risk of disability and to make work more attractive to older workers, and more general consultancy support aimed at improving general workplace policy making on age. A particular focus could be smaller firms without human resource functions.

Another approach is to increase labour market flexibility, which would enable workers to move to less demanding jobs.

---

[4] This perhaps accounts for the finding that, although awareness of the UK's Code of Practice on Age Diversity (http://www.agepositive.gov.uk) for employers has increased, there has been little change in practice (for an evaluation of the UK government's code see Goldstone and Jones, 2001, pp 22-3 and 25).

Tested/evaluated

An important deficiency in public policy has been the frequent absence of systematic evaluations of initiatives. A recent review concluded that there was little evidence on which types of public programmes work for older workers (Fay, 1996, p 26). While some results appear encouraging, questions remain regarding why initiatives are effective and whether there are significant deadweight effects. The literature on the impact of employment programmes more generally is limited by the previous absence of programmes targeting older workers or their inclusion in more general programmes. The UK has perhaps done more than other countries in terms of the evaluation of initiatives.

Long-term, consistent and positive

With the erosion of the certainty of fixed retirement ages, there is a need for increased support for older workers in managing risk in terms of career and retirement planning, and obtaining advice and guidance regarding job-seeking and training. At the same time, in order to help people to plan their futures, there is a need for clarity and consistency in terms of social security provision and pension policies.

There is also a need to get the incentive structure right and to link this to employment policy so that older workers are encouraged and supported to remain economically active. Pension and employment policy must proceed together if optimal effects are to be achieved.

It is important that campaigns aimed at raising awareness are long term, consistent and positive in their messages. After a long period during which the emphasis of public policy has often been on retirement, it will perhaps not be surprising if employers and older workers are sceptical about the notion of 'active ageing'. After all, it is only recently that the benefits of early retirement have been actively promoted by trades unions and policy makers. Also, too frequently, population ageing is discussed in almost apocalyptic terms, but public discussion presented in this way – however well intentioned – may only serve to confirm negative stereotypes among employers and older workers themselves. It is perhaps of little surprise that older workers report that they face substantial barriers in the labour market when this is the message given by academics, policy makers and the media.

Consistency in the application of public policy on age and employment is essential. For example, in Germany, while the integration of older workers is being promoted, the social partners have negotiated agreements whereby a gradual retirement scheme has become a de facto early retirement scheme. Such practices will significantly diminish the effectiveness of attempts to promote the employment of older workers.

Even attempts to highlight the positive attributes of older workers run the risk of confirming age stereotypes. For example, their value as keepers of corporate memory (Access Economics Pty Ltd, 2001, p 8) is often presented as a positive advantage of recruiting or retaining older workers, yet some companies may consider corporate memory to be associated with caution and conservative thinking and see it as a disadvantage. In addition, those promoting the cause of older workers have also sometimes been tempted to compare 'old' with 'young', for instance, older workers are argued to be stronger in the areas of employer loyalty and work ethic (Access Economics Pty Ltd, 2001, pp 14-15). Such statements embed age stereotypes in an attempt to counter them.

References

Access Economics Pty Ltd (2001) *Population ageing and the economy*, Canberra: Commonwealth of Australia.

Auer, P. and Fortunay, M. (1999) *Ageing of the labour force in OECD countries: Economic and social consequences*, Geneva: ILO.

Campbell, J.C. (1992) *How policies change: The Japanese government and the aging society*, Princeton, NJ: Princeton University Press.

Council on the Ageing (2001) *Investing in the future: Australia's ageing workforce*, Melbourne: Council on the Ageing.

EC (European Commission) (1999) *Active ageing: Promoting a European society for all ages*, Brussels: EC DGV Employment and Social Affairs.

Eironline (European Industrial Relations Observatory On-line) (2001) 'Alliance for jobs agrees joint statement on training', http://www.eiro.eurofound.ie/2001/03/feature/DE0103213F.html.

Encel, S. (2000a) 'Later-life employment', *Journal of Ageing and Social Policy*, vol 11, no 4, pp 7-13.

Encel, S. (2000b) 'Mature age employment: a long-term cost to society', *Economic and Labour Relations Review*, vol 11, no 2, pp 233-45.

Fay, R.G. (1996) *Enhancing the effectiveness of active labour market policies: Evidence from programme evaluations in OECD countries*, Labour Market and Social Policy Occasional Papers No 18, Paris: OECD.

Fujimura, H. (2001) 'Revision of pension system and employment issues involving workers in their early 60s', *Japan Labour Bulletin*, July, pp 6-12.

Goldstone, C. and Jones, D. (2001) 'Evaluation of the code of practice on age diversity in employment', in Department for Education and Employment, *Age diversity: Summary of research findings*, Nottingham: DfEE Publications.

Gruber, J. and Wise, D. (1999) 'Social security, retirement incentives and retirement behaviour: an international perspective', *Employee Benefit Research Institute Issue Brief 209*, Washington, DC: Employee Benefit Research Institute.

Guillemard, A.-M. (1997) 'Re-writing social policy and changes within the life course organisation: a European perspective', *Canadian Journal on Aging*, vol 16, no 3, pp 441-64.

Hansson, R.O., DeKoekkoek, P.D., Neece, W.M. and Patterson, D.W. (1997) 'Successful aging at work: annual review, 1992-1996: the older worker and transitions to retirement', *Journal of Vocational Behaviour*, vol 51, pp 202-33.

Hornstein, Z., Encel, S., Gunderson, M. and Neumark, D. (2001) *Outlawing age discrimination: Foreign lessons, UK choices*, Bristol/York: The Policy Press/Joseph Rowntree Foundation.

Human Resource Development Bureau (2000) *Human resource development in Japan*, Tokyo: Ministry of Labour.

ILO (International Labour Office) (2000) *World Labour Report*, Geneva: ILO.

Iwata, K. (2001) 'Employment of older persons and policy development in Japan', JIL Workshop/Symposium 2001 – Toward Active Ageing in the 21st Century, Papers and Highlights, Tokyo: The Japan Institute of Labour.

Iwata, K. (2002) 'Policies for the employment of older persons in Japan', *Journal of Japanese Trade and Industry*, May-June, pp 12-16.

Jacobs, K., Kohli, M. and Rein, M. (1991) 'Testing the industry mix hypothesis of early exit', in M. Kohli, M. Rein, A.-M. Guillemard and H. van Gunsteren (eds) (1991) *Time for retirement: Comparative studies of early exit from the labour force*, Cambridge: Cambridge University Press.

Japan Labour Bulletin (2001a) 'One in four large firms call for voluntary retirement or carry out dismissals', vol 40, no 11, p 1.

Japan Labour Bulletin (2001b) 'Guidelines to abolish age limits in the revised employment measures law', vol 40, no 11, pp 4-5.

Japan Labour Bulletin (2001c) 'Summary of employment measures to deal with deterioration of the job market', vol 40, no 11, p 5.

Kimura, T. and Oka, M. (2001) 'Japan's current policy focus on longer employment for older people', in V.W. Marshall, W.R. Heinz, H. Krüger and A. Verma (eds) *Restructuring work and the lifecourse*, Toronto: University of Toronto Press.

Klös, H.-P. (undated) *Elderly workers and the labour market – Stylized facts and the need for labour market reforms*, Köln: Institut der Deutschen Wirtschaft.

Kohli, M., Rein, M., Guillemard, A.-M. and van Gunsteren, H. (1991) *Time for retirement: Comparative studies of early exit from the labour force*, Cambridge: Cambridge University Press.

Koshiro, K. (1996) 'Policies for a smoother transition from work to retirement', *Journal of Aging and Social Policy*, vol 8, no 2-3, pp 97-113.

Kramer, F.D. (2001) *Aging baby boomers in a new workforce development system*, Washington, DC: Employment and Training Administration, US Department of Labor.

Kramer, F.D. and Smith Nightingale, D. (2001) *Using the Workforce Investment Act to serve mature and older workers*, Washington, DC: Division of Older Worker Programs, Employment and Training Administration, US Department of Labor.

Leppel, K. and Heller Clain, S. (1995) 'The effect of increases in the level of unemployment on older workers', *Applied Economics*, no 27, pp 901-6.

Lindley, R.M., Wilson, R. and Villagomez, E. (1991) *Labour market prospects for the third age: Carnegie Inquiry into the third age*, Coventry: Institute for Employment Research.

McIntosh, B. (2001a) *Supervisor's guide: Managing aging workers*, Washington, DC: Employment and Training Administration, US Department of Labor.

McIntosh, B. (2001b) *An employer's guide to older workers*, Washington, DC: Employment and Training Administration, US Department of Labor.

Ministry for Social Affairs and Employment (undated) *The old age pension system in the Netherlands: A brief outline*, The Hague: Ministry for Social Affairs and Employment.

Ministry for Social Affairs and Employment (2001) *The preventive approach in a nutshell*, The Hague: Ministry for Social Affairs and Employment.

Naganawa, H. (2002) 'Re-employment of older white-collar workers', *Japan Labour Bulletin*, vol 41, no 2, pp 6-10.

National Senior Citizens Education and Research Center (undated) *Using public relations to market older workers*, Washington, DC: Employment and Training Administration, US Department of Labor.

National Senior Citizens Education and Research Center (1998) *Using motivation and training to increase job placements*, Washington, DC: Employment and Training Administration, US Department of Labor.

OECD (Organisation of Economic Co-operation and Development) (2001) *Employment outlook*, Paris: OECD.

Poulos, S. and Smith Nightingale, D. (1997) *The aging baby boom: Implications for employment and training programs*, Washington, DC: Division of Older Worker Programs, Employment and Training Administration, US Department of Labor.

Queensland Government Department of Families (2000) 'A guide to retiring: planning your lifestyle', Brisbane: Queensland Government Department of Families.

Rix, S. (2001) 'Restructuring work in an aging America: what role for public policy', in V.W. Marshall, W.R. Heinz, H. Krüger and A. Verma (eds) *Restructuring work and the lifecourse*, Toronto: University of Toronto Press.

Sorsa, P. (1999) 'The Finnish national programme for ageing workers 1998-2002', Paper presented at the conference 'Active Strategies for an Ageing Workforce', Turku, Finland, 12-13 August.

Support Services International (undated) *Placing SCSEP enrollees in unsubsidized employment: A summary of best practice in successful programs*, Washington, DC: Employment and Training Administration, US Department of Labor.

Taylor, P. (2002) *Improving employment opportunities for older workers: Developing a policy framework*, Report to the European Commission, Prepared for the ninth EU–Japan Symposium 'Improving employment opportunities for older workers', Brussels, 21-22 March.

Taylor, P. and Walker, A. (1998) 'Policies and practices towards older workers: a framework for comparative research', *Human Resource Management Journal*, vol 8, no 3, pp 61-76.

Taylor, P., Encel, S. and Oka, M. (2002) 'Older workers – Trends and prospects', *Geneva Papers on Risk and Insurance*, vol 27, no 4, pp 512-33.

Trinder, C. (1989) *Employment after 55*, London: National Institute for Economic and Social Research.

Walker, A. (1999) 'The principals and potential of active ageing', Keynote introductory report for the European Commission Conference on Active Ageing, Brussels, 15-16 November.

Also available in the Transitions after 50 series
Published in association with the Joseph Rowntree Foundation

The pivot generation
Informal care and work after fifty

Ann Mooney and June Statham
This topical report explores how decisions about work are affected by caring responsibilities for people aged over 50. It draws together information from a variety of sources – an analysis of trends in employment at the household level over the past twenty years, a survey of employees and those who have recently retired in both a rural and an urban area, and over 30 in-depth interviews with people over 50 – to examine the extent of caring responsibilities and how they affect choices about the timing of retirement or reducing hours of work.

Paperback £11.95 tbc ISBN 1 86134 402 3

Early retirement and income in later life

Pamela Meadows
There is growing concern about the tendency for retirement from paid employment to take place before state pension age. One of the uncertainties is whether people who retire early have sufficient financial resources to support themselves through possibly thirty or more years of retirement. This report compares the financial position of people in the current pensioner population who retired early with their counterparts who retired at state pension age. *Early retirement and income in later life* will be of interest to all those studying, researching or working in the area of pensions and retirement.

Paperback £10.95 ISBN 1 86134 442 2

Income in later life
Work history matters

Elena Bardasi and Stephen Jenkins
Until now, little has been known about the relationships between older people's incomes and their work history patterns, and how these are mediated by other factors such as gender, partnerships, ill-health and disability. This report draws on data from the British Household Panel Survey to fill these gaps. The report is one of the few UK studies about incomes in later life that uses longitudinal data as well as information about work histories. It will be of interest to researchers and policy analysts who study incomes in later life, retirement and work careers.

Paperback £12.95 ISBN 1 86134 401 5

Outlawing age discrimination
Foreign lessons, UK choices

Zmira Hornstein, Sol Encel, Morley Gunderson and David Neumark
The UK is committed to legislating against age discrimination in employment and, under the EC Directive on Equal Treatment in Employment and Occupation, is expected to have legislation in place by December 2003. This important study looks at what can usefully be learned from other countries' experiences and analyses the options for the UK. It identifies legislation against age discrimination in employment in 13 countries, and looks in detail at Australia, Canada and the United States where legislation has been established for some time.

Paperback £14.95 ISBN 1 86134 354 X

Forging a new future
The expereinces and expectations of people leaving paid work over 50

Helen Barnes, Jane Parry amd Jane Lakey
Over one third of people over the age of 50 and under 65 are no longer in paid work. For some, this is a positive choice that allows them freedom to choose how to spend their time. For others, who may not have chosen to leave work, their options may be limited by income, health, caring responsibilities, or where they live.

Paperback £11.95 ISBN 1 86134 447 3

Transitions from work to retirement
Developing a new social contract

Chris Phillipson
People over the age of 50 now make up a significant proportion of the UK population. Transitions in this age group are increasingly complex, with work-based identities running alongside, or being interchanged with, leisure, caring, volunteering, and related activities. This report provides a detailed overview of the various transitions affecting people in their fifties and beyond.

Paperback £11.95 ISBN 1 86134 457 0

For further information about these and other titles published by The Policy Press, please visit our website at: www.policypress.org.uk or telephone +44 (0)117 954 6800
To order, please contact:
Marston Book Services
PO Box 269
Abingdon
Oxon OX14 4YN
UK Tel: +44 (0)1235 465500
Fax: +44 (0)1235 465556
E-mail: direct.orders@marston.co.uk